HOW TO
GROW YOUR LAW FIRM

A client-centric approach to being more profitable, in-demand, and highly reputable

Including:
The 7-Step
Growth
Blueprint

GERALD CHAIT

RƎTHINK PRESS

First published in Great Britain 2019
by Rethink Press (www.rethinkpress.com)

© Copyright Gerald Chait

Contents

Disclaimer

The contents of this book are informational in nature only. Content is not to be taken as instructional and is not given as legal, ethical or tax advice by either the author, publisher or anyone associated with this book. While best efforts have been taken to ensure the accuracy of the contents at time of publication, neither the author nor the publisher shall be held liable for any loss, however it may arise, or incidental or consequential damages caused directly or indirectly from the use of or reliance on the contents of this book. The results of marketing initiatives cannot be guaranteed.

This book is general in nature and may refer to marketing strategies that are restricted or prohibited under the legislation applicable to your specific business operations. To ensure your marketing initiatives do not breach any relevant legislation, or conflict with rules of your law society or association, it is important you seek your own independent legal advice from an appropriately qualified representative.

Introduction

A partner of a large firm commented that until recently, he had no idea how much marketing had developed over the years, and how it is now a lot more scientific and revenue-generating than he had ever imagined. He had always mistakenly considered marketing to be fluffy, pretty pictures and a cost centre to an organisation.

This made me realise that he isn't unique, and that many people with a limited knowledge of marketing would share similar views. As such, they would be unaware that professional, ethical and client-centric marketing not only benefits potential clients, but can generate extensive growth opportunities for firms.

Who this book is for

I have written this book for owners, partners, managers and lawyers in medium-sized and smaller law firms who wish to win more clients and grow profitability in the context of an increasingly competitive and changing environment. It is for skilled legal professionals who recognise they can achieve considerable improvements to both their business and personal wellbeing by embracing change, but who need guidance on what to embrace and how to embrace it. If any of this describes you, this book is dedicated to providing you with the information you need to understand modern marketing, so that you can ignite the growth of your firm.

The first step in becoming more profitable, in demand and highly reputable is recognising that the industry is changing rapidly and you can no longer rely solely on traditional business practices to prosper and grow.

Change can be difficult, and for this reason, many larger law firms engage specialists to help develop their business and marketing strategies. By reading this book and understanding the principles and methodologies it shares, you can develop strategies and tactics that outperform even the largest law firms with the greatest resources.

While the strategies, tactics and methodologies discussed in the book are relevant to most law firms, they are of greatest value if you practise the following law:

- Administrative
- Bankruptcy and insolvency
- Building and construction
- Community

- Competition and consumer
- Conveyancing
- Commercial
- Discrimination
- Dispute resolution
- Domestic violence
- Education
- Employment and HR
- Estate planning
- Family
- General practice
- Immigration
- Information technology
- Intellectual property
- International
- Media and communications
- Mediation
- Medicine and health
- Partnerships
- Personal injury and accident compensation
- Property

I am a highly successful marketer with extensive experience in growing businesses and have written this practical book to provide you with relevant information every step of the way.

The structure of the book

The book is divided into four sections:

- Section 1: The Legal Industry Today
- Section 2: Fundamentals of Modern Marketing
- Section 3: The Marketing Ecosystem
- Section 4: Executing A Modern Marketing Plan

I recommend that you read the book from front to back. The chapters build on each other, with the final three chapters tying together the information you will have learned throughout the book.

General rules about solicitors' advertising

It would be insufficient to discuss marketing strategies, methodologies and activities without reference to legislation or rules that may apply to advertising and the marketing of legal services. I refer to examples of legislation in effect in Australia, but please note this is not an exhaustive list and is for illustrative purposes only. It is important that any marketing and advertising initiatives you undertake comply with legislation, rules and guidelines relevant to your specific situation.

The Australian Consumer Law (ACL) (Cth)[1] is national legislation that covers 'any business or professional

---

1. www.legislation.gov.au/Details/C2017C00375

activity' and is therefore, in my opinion, pertinent to law firms. The ACL prohibits false, misleading and deceptive conduct and representations.

The Australian Solicitors' Conduct Rules 2015[2] also include references to advertising and marketing by legal practices. These references relate to false, misleading, deceptive, offensive and prohibited activity, as well as rules around the use of the words 'accredited specialist' or derivatives of those words. These words must only be used by solicitors who are accredited in the relevant speciality by their professional association. The Legal Services Council made the rules under the Legal Profession Uniform Law on 26 May 2015.[3]

The current Rules commenced in Victoria (VIC) and New South Wales (NSW) on 1 July 2015 and have been adopted in Queensland (QLD), South Australia (SA) and the Australian Capital Territory (ACT).[4]

---

2. www.lawcouncil.asn.au/files/web-pdf/Aus_Solicitors_Conduct
   _Rules.pdf
3. https://legislation.nsw.gov.au/#/view/regulation/2015/244/part2
   /divlawpractic/rule36
   www.legislation.gov.au/Details/C2017C00375
   www.lawsociety.com.au/practising-law-in-NSW/ethics-and
   -compliance/regulatory-compliance/advertising-legal-services
   www.qls.com.au/Knowledge_centre/Ethics/Resources
   /Advertising/What_are_the_rules_about_solicitors%E2%80
   %99_advertising_generally
   www.legislation.nsw.gov.au/regulations/2015-244.pdf
4. www.lawcouncil.asn.au/policy-agenda/regulation-of-the
   -profession-and-ethics/australian-solicitors-conduct-rules

In Western Australia (WA) there are similar rules under the Legal Profession Conduct Rules 2010, Part 7 – Miscellaneous.[5]

Another example from Australia covers the advertising of personal injury services. In the ACT, NSW, SA, VIC and Tasmania (TAS) there is currently no prohibition on the advertising of personal injury services, but such advertising is restricted in the Northern Territory (NT) (Legal Profession Act)[6] and WA (Civil Liability Act 2002),[7] and is prohibited in QLD (The Personal Injuries Proceedings Act 2002)[8] (PIPA).

We will discuss practical examples of personal injury services marketing in this book, but please be aware that these marketing initiatives may not be permitted in all states and territories of Australia, particularly NT, WA and QLD.

---

5. www.lawsocietywa.asn.au/wp-content/uploads/2015/10/Legal
    -Profession-Conduct-Rules-2010.pdf
6. https://lawsocietynt.asn.au/legal-profession-regulation.html
    ?id=50
    https://legislation.nt.gov.au/LegislationPortal/~/link.aspx?_id=
    9D17FD731A4549ACBDCCED1B01CF157C&_z=z
7. https://legislation.wa.gov.au/legislation/statutes.nsf/main
    _mrtitle_149_homepage.html
8. https://legislation.qld.gov.au/view/pdf/2017-03-01/act-2002-024

SECTION 1

The Legal Industry Today

CHAPTER 1
An Industry In Transformation

Introduction

The legal industry is experiencing a level of disruption that would have been difficult to predict just a few years ago. This disruption is having a considerable impact on the structure, traditions, customs and operations of the industry, and the livelihoods of many small and medium-sized law firms.

The disruption is being driven by rapid advances in technology, structural change and increasing competition.

Technology is powering:

- The formation of online services, both do it yourself (DIY) and full-service
- An increase in global firms

- Improved efficiencies from the adoption of artificial intelligence (AI)

Structural changes include:

- The emergence of multidisciplinary firms
- Growth of highly specialised niche firms
- Mergers, acquisitions and business investments
- Non-lawyers/technologists providing traditional legal services

Increasing competition coming from:

- An oversupply of lawyers

The rich traditions and customs of the legal industry – its very fabric – are being challenged. However, with challenge comes opportunity, and the opportunities are significant.

While being a great lawyer was once sufficient to achieve enormous growth, wealth and success, today, an understanding of the principles of marketing is crucial. Complementing legal skills with business and marketing skills helps lawyers differentiate them-selves, improve their reputation, attract clients and compete successfully in an increasingly competitive environment.

Drivers of transformation

The legal profession is undergoing massive disruption that is impacting on the structure, traditions and operations of the industry, as well as the livelihoods of many small and medium-sized law firms. While there has already been significant transformation, it has even been suggested that we will experience more change over the next twenty years than we have seen in the last two hundred.[9] While this accelerating pace of change is creating opportunities for many lawyers, it is also presenting challenges for other highly skilled professionals who have operated successfully for many years, but are now unsure how to adapt and prosper in this new world.

There are three key factors driving the disruption: technology, structural change and increasing competition.

While the industry continues to transform itself internally, the availability of information on the internet – information that was once exclusively available through traditional law firms – has shifted more control to the client than ever before. To survive, legal professionals need to be proactive and adapt to this changing landscape. This means they will require skills beyond law.

---

9. Richard Susskind, 'Change Now' (24 June 2015) *The Canadian Bar Association National Magazine* www.nationalmagazine.ca /Blog/June-2015/Change-now.aspx

'It is not the most intellectual of the species that survives; it is not the strongest that survives; but the species that survives is the one that is able best to adapt and adjust to the changing environment in which it finds itself.'

– Leon C Megginson[10]

Without a perpetual funnel of new leads and clients, even the best lawyers will struggle to survive. As with all businesspeople today, it is therefore critical that lawyers have an understanding of the principles of marketing.

TECHNOLOGY

Technology is one of the greatest drivers of change, and it is finding its way into the legal profession at an exponential rate. Its rapid adoption is being driven by internal and external pressure to reduce costs, lower fees, improve efficiencies and acquire more clients.

Online (cloud) solutions such as document management, practice management, web conferencing and AI are facilitating the growth of globalisation, DIY services and low-cost full-service online providers.

---

10. This quote is often attributed to Charles Darwin. However, more recent investigations suggest it was originally incorporated into a speech by Leon C Megginson, a Louisiana State University business professor.

While the impact of technology has wide-reaching consequences, it also presents significant opportunities for those who adapt and embrace it. No longer does cost or complexity limit it to large firms; most technology today is easy to use and affordable for smaller practices to adopt.

Online DIY and full-service online firms

Websites such as LegalVision, LawPath, Virtual Legal and Sprint Law are examples of a new generation of legal services made possible by technology. Some newer solutions provide a comprehensive online service, while others are more limited, for example creating legal documents via a self-service model. Online services are low-cost and can be fully or partially automated. For example, online document creation can be fully automated – a client simply answers relevant questions, and the software generates the complete document. In other cases, the client purchases a low-cost (sometimes free) document and inputs their own relevant information into it.

Global firms

Technology has driven down the cost and increased the ease of communicating globally in real time. Email, the internet, online meetings, webinars, video links and cloud-based software are easy and often free to use, enabling businesses and customers to communicate and meet with each other from anywhere in the world at any time. This is resulting in more businesses trading globally and creating the need for legal firms to operate across national borders.

AI

Over the past few years, we have started hearing about AI becoming more prevalent in the legal industry. Essentially, true AI is the ability for a machine to learn, make decisions based on this learning, and do what once only a human could do.

While true AI is still in its infancy, simple AI applications are entering the legal industry. These are generally related to document management and research. AI is faster and more efficient than having humans manually sort through every piece of content to locate appropriate documentation.

As AI technology continues to develop, it is likely to become more commonplace, valuable and effective across a broader range of law firms.

INDUSTRY STRUCTURE AND OPERATIONS

The structure of the legal industry and the way it operates is also transforming rapidly. Traditionally, law firms operated in a regulated market and were well protected. They maintained a hierarchical organisation structure and required minimal innovation in order to prosper. As legislation relating to how law firms can advertise and market their services becomes more relaxed, this drives greater competition within the profession.

As a result, there is a significant amount of innovation occurring, including the emergence of multidisciplinary firms, mergers and acquisitions, and even non-lawyers providing services that have historically been the domain of traditional law firms.

Multidisciplinary firms

Where once a client engaged with a law firm for their legal needs, an accounting firm for their finance needs, and a business consultant for strategic support, this is no longer always the case. Larger, often global, accounting firms started adding legal services to their portfolios, then larger law firms added business consulting services, including strategy, HR and financial services. More recently, smaller law firms have also been adding to their services and offering strategic consulting and implementation support across a range of disciplines.

While this is an alternative strategy to specialising or niching through deep expertise in a particular area of law, proponents of the multidisciplinary model believe they are able to provide greater value through a 360 degree understanding of their clients' businesses.

Highly specialised firms

While many law firms offer a wide variety of legal services, others are specialising in niche areas. These firms are experts in a particular area of law and can benefit from lower overheads, greater authority and improved efficiencies.

Mergers, acquisitions and investments

Mergers, acquisitions and investments are additional factors in the ever-changing legal environment. Firms generally make the decision to merge with, acquire or invest in another firm for one or more of the following reasons:

- To capitalise on changes in the industry more quickly and cost effectively, eg to achieve globalisation and multinational representation
- To expand the range of legal or multidisciplinary services they can offer
- To create a strategic competitive advantage by owning unique or well-developed technology
- To reduce overall costs and increase profits
- To provide greater resources for growth

Non-lawyers/technologists providing traditional legal services

Various types of legal work have been performed by non-lawyers for many years, so there is nothing new in this. Examples include conveyancing, tax advice and company registrations.

However, over the last ten years, we have started seeing technology companies building solutions and offering online legal services, with or without their own internal lawyers, directly to the end client. This is creating even greater competition in the profession, altering client expectations and lowering the perceived value of expert lawyers, resulting in pressure to reduce fees. This trend is likely to continue into the future.

INCREASING COMPETITION

Competition can be defined as lawyers competing for the same clients in order to generate revenue.

Oversupply of lawyers[11]

Australian universities are pumping out an oversupply of graduates each year, and this seems to be a trend throughout the English-speaking world. More and

---

11. www.smh.com.au/national/law-of-the-jungle-lawyers-now-an -endangered-species-20141011-114u91.html

more articles and reports are addressing this issue and the difficulties it is creating for not only the graduates themselves, who find it increasingly hard to find employment, but the profession as a whole.

There are currently approximately 75,000 lawyers in Australia. An oversupply of capacity dilutes demand, erodes profitability, and results in underutilised staff.

With educational institutions generating income based on the number of students they take on, there are also concerns that high standards may be being relaxed in the interests of student numbers. In an increasingly competitive environment, law schools that give limited attention to developing business and marketing skills may be further exacerbating the problem.

The large number of lawyers, increasing efficiencies and more informed clients demanding greater value for their dollar are all putting pressure on fees.

The strategies and models described in this book can help remove the need to compete against low fees. In fact, they can actually help firms increase fees by becoming highly reputable, well known and sought after.

Skills beyond law

Lawyers have traditionally operated in a somewhat controlled environment, relying heavily upon word of mouth to generate client acquisition. They enjoyed higher profit margins, lower competition, and minimal disruption. Lawyers could focus on doing their best legal work, confident in the knowledge that the next client would arrive as needed.

Up until the mid-1990s there were tight restrictions on how they could promote their services and generate new business. Working in this relatively controlled environment, lawyers had little need to learn business skills outside of their profession.

Likewise, law schools had little need to introduce business management, sales and marketing subjects into their courses. This has resulted in many lawyers now lacking a solid understanding of marketing. Therefore, some have not known how to proactively market their services, while others have held on to a misguided belief that marketing their services lowers their reputation in the eyes of their peers and clients.

With a little information and guidance, more lawyers are now becoming aware that ethical client-centric marketing can actually increase their reputation, improve their client service and grow their practice.

An understanding of professional marketing is no longer an option, but rather critical in today's changing environment.

THE WORLD IS MOVING ON

I've often heard people use the phrase, 'The world has passed me by'. At the speed the world moves today, this can happen in what seems to be a single blink of the eye.

To be successful, innovative lawyers recognise they need to embrace change, but more importantly, ensure they are continually learning and keeping abreast of latest developments.

It requires a determined effort to continuously upskill, but as the legal industry continues to be disrupted, adaptation, flexibility and new skills become paramount. We've moved into an era where lifelong learning and continual adaptation are necessary parts of doing business.

Outside of law, it is important to keep sales, marketing and technical skills up to date. This often requires a major shift in thinking and an open mind to learning.

WORKING ON VS WORKING IN THE FIRM

This is an age-old problem that comes up time and time again. Legal professionals often focus their time and energy on activities that generate an immediate income, for example, doing the paid client work personally. This is known as working in the business.

The opportunity cost of personally doing all of the work is that it does not allow legal professionals time to work *on* the firm beyond its existing client base – in other words, they don't allocate time to marketing, developing business growth plans or acquiring new clients. Firms fail to grow as they should; principals and partners become stuck in a relentless rat race that drains their energy and stifles innovation. In the long term, working in rather than on the business is a lost opportunity and a significant barrier to growth.

Working on the business includes activities outside of practising law that set the firm up for long-term growth and success. It is only when legal professionals step outside of their business and look in that they can clearly identify growth opportunities.

The old saying 'Can't see the forest for the trees' is particularly appropriate when 100% of a lawyer's time is dedicated to daily client work. It's clearly not feasible to drop all paid client work to work on the business, but by making time each week to work on business development, lawyers will maximise their chances of delivering long-term success, often in a more enjoyable environment.

Finding the balance between working in and working on the business can be difficult; it requires commitment and planning. Working on the business could include the entire team meeting for a couple of hours each week to discuss ideas and work on growth opportunities, or it could be a sole operator developing and executing growth plans. One way to free up some time without losing paid work is to delegate tasks to others. By doing this in a manner that minimises the impact on current work, legal professionals can simultaneously plan and execute a growth strategy. It may require outsourcing some work in the short term, hiring additional in-house resources, or even declining work that may not be a perfect short-term fit. It may mean engaging with third-party specialists to help strategise and execute. However, it is essential that all legal professionals allow time to work on as well as in their firms.

Summary

There is currently significant disruption occurring in the legal industry. The rate of change has never been greater, and it is expected to continue increasing exponentially.

Disruption is being driven by rapid advances in technology, structural change and increasing competition.

Technology is powering:

- The formation of online services, both do it yourself (DIY) and full-service
- An increase in global firms
- Improved efficiencies from the adoption of artificial intelligence (AI)

Structural changes include:

- The emergence of multidisciplinary firms
- Growth of highly specialised niche firms
- Mergers, acquisitions and business investments
- Non-lawyers/technologists providing traditional legal services

Increasing competition coming from:

- An oversupply of lawyers

It is critical, therefore, that lawyers have an understanding of the principles of marketing. By complementing legal skills with business and marketing skills, lawyers can differentiate themselves, improve their reputation, attract clients and compete more successfully. These exciting changes to the legal profession are delivering fantastic opportunities for proactive lawyers who embrace the new era.

This change is not exclusive to the legal industry; new generations are growing up in an entirely different world from just ten years ago. For the legal industry, however, the effects of the changes may be more pronounced, the reason being that in addition to operational changes, the industry's rich traditions and customs are being challenged. As a result, the old ways are no longer sustainable.

With change comes opportunity, and the opportunities have never been greater, but harvesting them requires a change in mindset. To excel in the legal industry today, lawyers must embrace change and welcome the new world with open arms.

Now is the time to go forth and conquer.

SECTION 2

Fundamentals of Modern Marketing

CHAPTER 2

Professional, Ethical Marketing

Introduction

As a professional marketer, I occasionally come across people who believe marketing is akin to selling snake oil – a bad, manipulative industry they need to steer well clear of. These people have often formed their opinions through negative personal experiences, such as persistent telemarketers calling at dinner time or, in the old days, their letterbox overflowing with junk mail.

There is also an anti-marketing mindset among some lawyers who feel:

- Marketing is outside of their comfort zones
- Their time is better spent on legal work
- Marketing violates traditions and professional ethics

- Legal work comes from referrals; marketing would be a waste of their time, effort and money

This book is about professional and ethical marketing. It is about growing a law firm by putting the client first, developing strong relationships and engaging with people to help them solve their problems. It is about law firms becoming more profitable by providing a highly efficient client-centric service.

Client-centric marketing – solving problems

Professional marketing today is about putting the potential client first; it is about understanding their issues and problems, and delivering solutions that solve these problems. Of course, you still need to demonstrate to potential clients that you are the best person to solve their problems, and you achieve this by creating appropriate communications and interactions that share knowledge and position you as an authority.

Each interaction with your potential client needs to be personal, timely and relevant. Always approach marketing from a 'What's in it for the client?' or 'How is this helping the client?' point of view, rather than 'What's in it for me?' or simply listing your services. A list of services doesn't engage potential clients emotionally or position you as the expert they can trust.

What is professional, ethical marketing?

When a person or business needs legal advice and support, it is generally because they have a problem or issue that needs solving. It may simply be that they require help drafting a non-disclosure agreement (NDA) or a privacy policy for their website, or it may be more serious, such as a medical malpractice or family dispute. Whatever their issue, they require the services of an experienced lawyer to help them solve it.

If they've never needed this type of legal support and don't have connections, they won't know whom to approach or whom they can trust to help them. They have a very real problem, potentially they have time pressures, and they simply don't know whom to turn to, which often causes them anxiety, stress and frustration. They need someone who will give them the confidence and reassurance that they'll receive the right advice at the right price.

Professional, ethical marketing is about helping potential clients find you when they need you, allowing them to move through a process that gives them confidence that you are the right person to help them solve their problem. The 7-Step Growth Blueprint process, which we will discuss in detail in Chapter 7, achieves this, thereby helping you grow your client base.

Professional marketing continues beyond the lead acquisition and onboarding stages. It results in a client having a positive, delightful experience working with you, and ensures that when someone they know needs your services, they will sing your praises and recommend you without hesitation.

Implementing professional, ethical marketing will win you more clients by developing trusting relationships with potential clients. It will help your firm become recognised as the highly reputable go-to firm in your particular field of expertise. When distilled to its lowest level, ethical marketing is about doing the right thing – being factual, honest, transparent, non-manipulative, fair and compliant with legislation and the rules of relevant professional bodies. This creates strong customer engagement, trust and confidence.

Professional industries such as the legal industry once relied on referrals. Today, it is becoming harder to sustain or grow a business on referrals alone. It now requires you to position yourself and your business to be found by someone requiring your services. Once they have become aware of you and have interacted with you, they can decide for themselves whether they would like to engage your services on an ongoing basis.

Modern digital technologies such as websites, search engine optimisation (SEO), AdWords, social media, blogs, display advertising and marketing automation make it efficient, easy and cost effective to employ strategies that enable potential clients to find you. We will discuss these technologies and associated methodologies in more detail throughout the book.

The anti-marketing mindset

In the early 1990s, the Australian government committed to reforming the legal profession for the purpose of introducing greater competition, increased choice and improved services. It felt that relaxing restrictions on advertising and promotions would help achieve these objectives.

In July 1996, the Australian Federal Bureau of Consumer Affairs released guidelines relating to the advertising of legal services. These were part of far-reaching reforms that included a significant relaxation of restrictions on a lawyer's ability to advertise their services. From that time, legal-service providers, in most parts of Australia, were able to advertise in a similar way to other businesses.

While many successful and progressive lawyers adopted marketing strategies and stepped up their game, others held on to negative perceptions of marketing. They didn't realise that done well, marketing actually helps their clients and potential clients, which in turn helps them to build their businesses.

Unless potential clients are made aware that you can help them solve their problems, it is unlikely they will engage your services, and without clients paying a fee for the services you provide, you don't have a sustainable business. Therefore, it is essential that potential clients become aware of your services, specialist knowledge and expertise.

Let's now have a look at how some lawyers are limiting their success through an anti-marketing mindset.

MARKETING IS OUTSIDE THEIR COMFORT ZONE

Marketing is not taught at law school, and many practising lawyers don't have the time or desire to understand exactly what marketing is, how it works, or the value it can bring to their practice. Other lawyers do have an appreciation of marketing, but simply don't know where or how to get started. Either reason can lead to lawyers shying away from marketing altogether.

As marketing is often critical to the success of a business, it is important that lawyers who run law firms either take an active role in managing their own marketing, or work closely with a trusted professional marketer to help grow their practice.

A BELIEF THAT THEIR TIME IS BETTER SPENT ON LEGAL WORK

Generating an income by allocating time to client work for a fee is fundamental to business success. Without it, a business's survival is doomed. However, as we have already discussed, lawyers also need to allocate time to work on the business for its long-term growth and success. This is just as important as working on client jobs.

Today, being a good lawyer alone is not enough.

A BELIEF THAT MARKETING VIOLATES TRADITIONS AND ETHICS

Some lawyers, particularly those who operated in an era when marketing was prohibited by outdated professional rules, still believe that marketing is akin to trickery and deception. They may even believe that if they undertake marketing activities, they will be seen by their peers and clients as unsuccessful.

In reality, nothing could be further from the truth. The legal industry today is more competitive than it has ever been. Leading businesses in virtually any industry place a great deal of emphasis on marketing to maintain their success and grow.

Marketing that reinforces positive references, whether they be via word of mouth or comments on blog posts, review sites and social media, has the ability to propel a legal firm to significantly greater success. However, marketing is not, and never has been, compensation for an inferior product or service. Real clients leaving negative reviews, blogs posts or social media comments will render any marketing efforts worthless. The trick is to get the product and service levels right first, and then leverage them with high-quality marketing strategies.

There are plenty of ethical, professional marketers as well as the unscrupulous, just as there are good, honest lawyers along with the not so squeaky clean. Simply stay away from the unscrupulous marketers. They can

33

generally be recognised by their claims – if their offering sounds too good to be true, it probably is.

Professional, ethical marketing does not violate traditions; in fact, it helps support clients, and can mean you provide a superior service to them.

A BELIEF THAT LEGAL WORK ALWAYS COMES FROM REFERRALS

Referrals are an important source of business, but they are not the only possible source. Traditionally, when firms were not permitted to advertise their services, most lawyers' business came from referral networks.

Referrals can come from other lawyers or current/ past clients. When they are predominantly generated through other lawyers, maintaining good relationships with those lawyers is in itself a form of marketing. When referrals are predominantly from past clients, effective marketing could increase these referrals even further.

However, when a law firm needs to grow revenue and profitability, referrals and word of mouth are unlikely to be sufficient. Clients will need to be sourced through other channels as well, and effective marketing is the power that drives those channels.

For example, let's assume a law firm needs to grow by

15 to 20% per year, but it is already receiving the maximum number of referrals possible through its network. Its growth will therefore need to come from new marketing initiatives. Innovative, proactive and dynamic firms, with partners seeking continual improvement in their business and personal lives, implement professional marketing activities to deliver growth above and beyond referrals.

Marketing and sales

Every business needs revenue to survive, and sales and marketing are both activities designed to help generate that revenue. While they are related, they are also very different.

Marketing generally involves top and middle of the sales funnel activities, such as generating visitors to your website, converting them into leads (eg a website visitor who has provided their name and some form of contact details), and them finally becoming a marketing qualified lead (more deeply engaged than a lead).

Sales activities generally involve middle and bottom of funnel activities, such as creating sales qualified leads (marketing qualified leads that salespeople feel are ready for direct follow up), opportunities (sales qualified leads that salespeople have contacted and rated as highly likely to become clients), and clients (opportunities who have formally engaged your services).

While I have related sales activities to salespeople in the explanation above, it is important to recognise that lawyers, and especially partners in law firms, should be undertaking sales activities to win new clients.

MARKETING/LEAD GENERATION

ATTRACT
Potential client visits website

LOW

LEADS
Potential client provides contact details

MARKETING-QUALIFIED LEADS
Potential client has a problem/issue
we can solve and meets our client profile

SALES-QUALIFIED LEADS
Potential client is ready to commit

LEAD SCORE
Likelihood of becoming a client

OPPORTUNITIES
Initial consultation
with potential client

CLIENTS
Onboarding

HIGH

SALES/ONBOARDING

Figure 2.1: Sales Funnel

Developing your value proposition

Before you can even consider developing your marketing strategy, one of the first steps is to articulate your unique value proposition.

A unique value proposition is a clear articulation of who

your client is, the problems they have that you can solve, and your unique approach to solving them. There must be an element of uniqueness to differentiate the way you solve problems from how another lawyer would solve the same problems. In an industry experiencing oversupply and disruption, differentiation is critical to success. It sets you apart and helps you stand out in a mass of sameness. Lawyers need to have a unique and compelling value proposition and be able to answer the question 'So what do you do differently and how do you do it differently?'

Summary

Professional, ethical marketing is positive and helpful. It enables you to grow your law firm by doing the right thing for others, helping them solve their problems.

Some traditional lawyers perceive marketing as akin to selling snake oil, but modern professional and ethical marketing couldn't be further from this myth. Because traditional lawyers didn't tend to learn marketing at law school, they often don't realise how ethical and client-centric marketing actually provides a valuable service to potential clients while generating new business at the same time.

Ethical marketing does not violate professional traditions. Rather, it is a valuable component of an innovative firm's services. Marketing deals with the top and middle of the sales funnel, while sales focus on the middle and lower sections.

To stand out and be noticed, ensure you have articulated your value proposition and differentiated yourself from other 'me-too' lawyers. Having a unique, differentiated positioning in the market is critical to maximising long term success.

CHAPTER 3

Overcoming Industry Challenges

Introduction

In an environment where referrals are no longer enough, lawyers must attract new clients from other sources.

New clients will gravitate towards lawyers they know, like and trust. By executing the 7-Step Growth Blueprint and client-centric marketing strategies, you can maximise the number of potential clients who feel that they know, like and trust you. This approach also leverages technology to provide a twenty-four hours a day, 365 days a year response to enquiries without you having to do so manually – an important factor in today's 'immediate fulfilment' environment.

In a similar manner to the legal industry, the marketing industry has also experienced major disruption brought about by technology. Marketing today can be divided into two main categories: 'traditional marketing' and 'modern digital marketing'. Traditional marketing includes non-digital media, such as magazine, newspaper, television and radio advertising. Messaging is impersonal, less timely, less targeted, and less precise.

With modern digital marketing, you can identify potential clients with pinpoint accuracy, and then communicate with each of them in a personal one-to-one manner. Communications with them will be relevant, timely, engaging and educational, and results will be highly measurable.

Digital marketing, through the development and distribution of content, will also enable you to become known as an expert in your field.

How marketing overcomes current industry challenges

People buy from people they get to know, like and trust. This is important to understand when it comes to professional services marketing, where the product and the provider are essentially one and the same. Product marketing is somewhat different in that consumers can purchase an identical product from a number of different sources. For example, a particular brand and model of laptop computer will be the same irrespective of whom you purchase it from. With professional services marketing, no two solutions will be the same. The end solution is a product of the individual provider, their skill, personality, style, pricing etc.

As a lawyer, you need to stand out from the crowded market, positioning yourself as the expert who will achieve the very best result for your client. By developing a reputation as the best in the industry, you will ensure potential clients gravitate towards you. Irrespective of new low-cost entrants, offshore providers and multidisciplinary firms, you can become the go-to provider in your niche.

While there will be a section of the market for whom lower-cost, lower engagement online services will be sufficient, as the complexity of a client's needs and the associated risks increase, they will require deeper levels of specialisation, experience, and a more personalised service. These clients will be happy to pay more if they are comfortable that the outcome will be right for them.

As a lawyer, position yourself as the most highly regarded and experienced person who will provide the time, care and skill to solving the client's problem. Marketing helps you to become known as that person and be found when a potential client needs your services. This results in you being able to stand out from the sea of sameness, attract more clients, and increase fees and charges.

Ultimately, marketing will help you run a highly sought-after, profitable law firm with a strong reputation.

Traditional and digital marketing

TRADITIONAL

Traditional marketing is any form of marketing that does not utilise digital technologies. It is often thought of as old school, but used strategically, it can be extremely effective. In most situations, a combination of traditional marketing and digital marketing generates the greatest results.

Common forms of traditional marketing include print advertising, direct mail, events, public relations (PR), and broadcast. Print advertising is any marketing activity utilising printed paper. This includes basic flyers through to high-quality multipage brochures and catalogues, outdoor signage, newspapers and magazines. Despite digital technologies, print marketing has continued to develop and is still an important component of many advertising and promotional strategies.

Broadcast marketing includes marketing activities conducted through media such as radio and television. It takes many forms and is not limited to advertisements alone. Program sponsorships, live interviews and participation in business programs and documentaries all form part of broadcast marketing strategies.

Traditional marketing tools still play an important role in the overall marketing mix, and can in some situations be even more effective than digital marketing. Printed brochures, for example, are an excellent way to present an intangible service as a tangible product solution that potential clients can relate to. Traditional marketing is, however, generally less customised and personalised.

DIGITAL

Digital marketing strategies utilise technologies and devices such as the internet, computers, mobile phones and digital outdoor advertising. They are typically executed through websites, blogs, search engines, email, social media, phone apps, eBooks, online display and search advertising, and marketing automation systems.

Digital marketing strategies can include both outbound and inbound tactics, which we will cover in detail in Chapter 4. The display ads that you see on websites as you browse the internet are examples of outbound digital tactics, while inbound digital tactics include relevant online content that is search engine optimised and found through Google or other searches, ie the potential client initiates the action which results in them becoming aware of your firm.

A key difference between digital marketing and traditional marketing is the number of free digital marketing solutions that can be taken advantage of. For example, as a lawyer, you may elect to write an article and post it to your LinkedIn profile and other relevant LinkedIn groups, or write a blog and optimise it to appear in

Google searches. Both of these can be very effective zero to low-cost marketing tactics.

Digital marketing has introduced a significantly more measurable and data-driven approach to marketing. Virtually everything in the digital environment can be tracked, measured and refined in real time, meaning that you can determine the performance and return on investment (ROI) of almost every activity accurately, and make changes to improve performance quickly and easily. Digital data helps improve your decision making and enables a high degree of precision marketing, allowing you to target and engage your ideal clients. The tools to do this are included within digital advertising platforms such as Google Ads and Facebook, as well as modern marketing automation solutions. Google Analytics is also a powerful free tool that enables you to measure the performance of your website.

This ability to measure performance is one of the greatest benefits of digital marketing over traditional marketing. Let's say, for example, you post an advertisement promoting your mediation services in the local print newspaper. You will have little idea who has acted as a result of seeing your ad. By contrast, you can precisely measure the results of an online ad, whether it targets people who have previously visited your website, or are new in the market and unaware of your firm. Not only can you measure statistics such as the number of people who have seen your advertisement, but you can measure the number of people who have clicked on it and visited your website or taken action because of it. You can also track the performance of your ad in generating leads and clients, and the actual cost per client acquired. Digital marketing, combined with the right analytics tools, allows you to track your clients back to their first digital exposure to your firm.

While you can use both traditional and digital marketing to attract potential clients to your firm, digital marketing is the foundation for deeper engagement and nurturing. Examples of digital engagement tactics include eBooks, video, text messages, automated messages direct to voicemail, online calculators, automated webinars, appointment setting, online chat etc.

There are many factors to consider when you're weighing up traditional versus digital marketing. However, in today's world, with changing buyer behaviours and new easy-to-use low-cost technologies, most marketing campaigns are formed on a digital-first strategy, complemented with traditional media as required.

When we think about the information sources potential clients will use to research law firms, it is highly likely that they will undertake a Google search rather than referring to a physical directory, as they would have done in the past. According to Google, online searches are now the number one method of researching and finding businesses. A digital presence is no longer an optional add on to a marketing strategy; today, it needs to form the foundation of the marketing strategy.

Your website is the centrepiece of your digital strategy, with most other digital marketing tactics leveraging and complementing it. Digital directories such as True Local, social media such as Facebook, video marketing, email marketing, and Google solutions such as AdWords, Analytics and Google My Business all form strong components of a digital marketing strategy that leverages your website.

Irrespective of whether you are dealing with one or 1,000 potential clients, you need to interact with every person uniquely. Your communications with them must be relevant, timely, engaging and educational.

Imagine as an example that you are a personal injury lawyer. A potential client has been injured in a motor vehicle accident. They Google 'car accident lawyer' and your details appear on Google's search engine results page (SERP). They click through to your website and read a blog on the steps to take immediately following a serious accident.

At this stage, they don't provide you with their contact details, but go on to view other personal injury lawyers' websites, all looking fairly similar. The next day, after having viewed ten websites, they are scrolling through their Facebook feed when an advert for your firm appears, offering them a valuable checklist and more in-depth information related to what they were reading on your blog. This is appealing to them, so they click on the ad and are taken to a landing page where they enter their name and email address to receive, via email, the additional content.

In your email to them, you include a link to other relevant content on your website. When they return to your site to view this content, you are able to track their behaviour, such as the pages they've visited and the articles they've read, and based on this, continue offering useful, relevant content.

They will come to recognise you as an expert in your field and will likely want to get in touch with you. You may have an online booking facility that allows them to view your availability and schedule a free initial consultation. Once they meet with you, there is an extremely high likelihood that they will engage your services and become a new client. While providing an excellent service to the potential client, you will have also differentiated yourself from competitors and earnt the potential client's trust and confidence.

Ten years ago, this type of automated, client-centric solution either did not exist, or was extremely costly and only available to the largest corporations. Today, it is within the reach of sole operators. The entire process is straightforward to implement, and the first time you personally become involved with the potential client is when they call or meet with you.

Today, not only does marketing help you to engage clients, but new tools and systems allow you to improve efficiencies and save time in the day-to-day operations of your firm. Let's assume you are ready to send your new client a fee schedule and letter of engagement. If you integrate your document management system with your marketing automation system, the system can automatically send a personalised document to the potential client for execution.

24/7 ACCESS AND AVAILABILITY

Ten years ago, a potential client may have seen an advert promoting your services. They may have tried to reach you on the telephone, but as you were tied up in a conference all day, they left a message with your practice manager. They did, however, manage to reach a competitor, and schedule a meeting with that competitor. They then decided to wait for the outcome of that meeting before deciding whether to speak with you.

You may have lost a potential client because you weren't able to respond immediately.

Modern marketing systems overcome this problem in many ways. You are essentially available to provide the information to the potential client 24/7, any day or week of the year, even public holidays. If they are still up at 1am, worrying about how they should solve their problem, you will be able to provide them with the relevant information, despite being off the grid and fast asleep.

The concept of the nine-to-five business day is all but gone. Clients don't just expect information at any hour of the day, many consider it standard practice. No one has time to wait days, or even hours; they want relevant information when they want it, and if they can't find it from you, they will seek alternatives – even at 1am.

Industry authority

Potential clients need confidence that the lawyer they're dealing with has the appropriate skills and expertise to offer the perfect solution to their problem. There are numerous ways to position yourself as the expert in your field and become the go-to person for both potential clients and other lawyers needing to refer clients on.

Being an industry authority in a particular area of law, displaying the highest level of ethics, integrity and expertise, will enable you to attract clients and charge premium fees. While it is not difficult to position yourself as an authority, it does take time and commitment.

Some of the most effective ways industry authorities position themselves as experts include:

- Presenting at conferences
- Being active in industry associations
- Hosting a regular podcast
- Sharing a regular blog
- Being active on social media
- Answering questions on social media and other forums
- Authoring a book

- Promoting and presenting webinars
- Media exposure
- Surrounding themselves with other like-minded industry authorities

Being an industry authority requires innovation. Try new things, share your successes, and make sure you're regarded as a leader. Being an industry authority isn't about holding on to information; it is about sharing your knowledge and assisting others whenever possible. Remember, if you don't share your knowledge, people won't be aware of your expertise and skills.

Sharing knowledge and educating others needs to become a key part of who you are professionally. In many ways, you will be a teacher. You could teach via blogging or a regular podcast, or offering yourself up for appropriate speaking engagements.

As an industry authority, you believe in yourself and your capabilities; you don't shy away from taking risks or working long, hard hours. When you position yourself as an industry authority, you accept the responsibility associated with it. Depending on your specific objectives, social media sites such as LinkedIn and Facebook offer untold opportunities to raise your profile.

Modern marketing has become both the lawyer and client's friend. By developing a reputation as the best in the industry, you will stand out from the crowded marketplace and become known, liked and trusted.

Developing a marketing strategy

Implementing a successful marketing strategy begins with understanding your business objectives and goals. You then design your marketing strategy to support your business objectives. For example, if your firm's objective is to grow client retention by 100% and new client acquisition by 20%, your strategy will be very different from a firm needing to grow acquisition by 100% and retention by 20%.

Too many businesses start their marketing journey by implementing tactics without referencing the bigger picture. This is like jumping into a car and driving without having a destination in mind; you'll drive all day, draining your energy, wearing out your tyres, and by the time you get out of the car, you may simply be back where you started, blaming the car for not arriving at a satisfactory destination.

So it is with marketing. Unless you know your business objectives, there is limited value in executing a marketing strategy or tactics.

A STRATEGIC MARKETING FRAMEWORK

Developing and executing a successful marketing strategy incorporates six steps:

1. Analyse your overall business objectives
2. Develop SMART marketing objectives

3. Develop a marketing strategy that aligns business and marketing objectives

4. Plan the optimum tactical approach

5. Execute with beautiful design and precision

6. Review results, report and refine

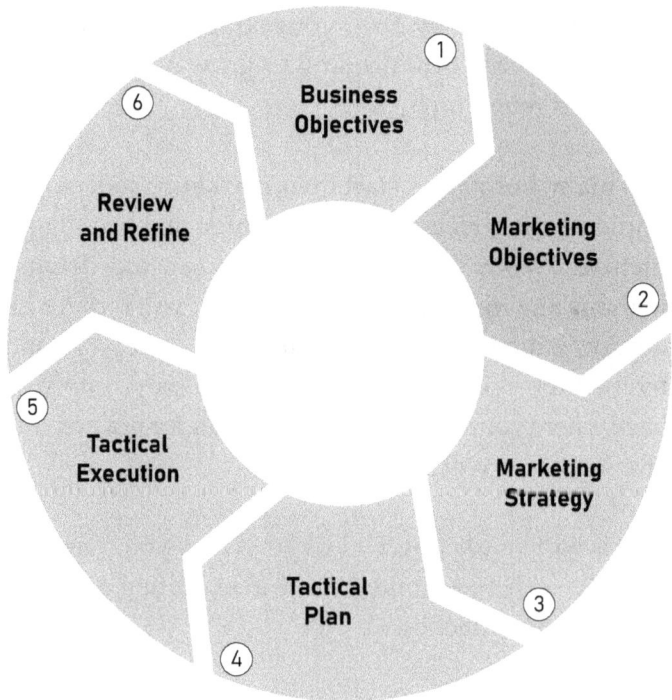

Figure 3.1: Strategic Marketing Framework

SMART MARKETING OBJECTIVES

Step two of the strategic marketing framework requires the development of SMART marketing objectives. A SMART objective is:

- **Specific:** the more specific your objective is, the more likelihood you have of achieving it.
- **Measurable:** in order to measure your progress, you need your goal to be quantifiable.
- **Achievable:** if the reality is that the objective is unachievable or unrealistic, eg the cost in time or effort is beyond what you can allocate, then you need to reassess the objective.
- **Relevant:** objectives must be relevant. For example, your objective might be to market both legal and accounting services, but if you have no accountants in your firm, and no budget for hiring or outsourcing to accountants, it is not a relevant objective at this point in time.
- **Timely:** objectives require timeframes in which to be achieved. Timeframes result in more concrete objectives and drive actions.

An example of a SMART objective could be to grow the number of motor vehicle accident injury cases you represent in Sydney by 15% year on year over the next two years. Many firms may set a primary objective with multiple secondary objectives.

Once you have established your firm's marketing objectives, you then design your marketing tactics to achieve them.

Summary

Modern digital marketing helps lawyers win more clients and grow profitability through highly relevant, targeted engagement, twenty-four hours per day, seven days per week, fifty-two weeks per year.

Digital marketing allows you to identify your potential clients, and then communicate with them in a personal, relevant, timely, engaging and educational manner. In addition, the results are measurable. Digital marketing through the development and distribution of content also enables you to become known as an expert in your field, increasing your credibility and, in turn, the demand for your services.

While traditional marketing is less precise and personal than modern digital marketing, including appropriate traditional tactics can add significant value to your overall marketing strategy.

Developing and executing a successful marketing strategy incorporates the following six steps:

1. Analyse your overall business objectives
2. Develop SMART marketing objectives
3. Develop a strategy that aligns business and marketing objectives
4. Plan the optimum tactical approach
5. Execute with beautiful design and precision
6. Review results, report and refine

CHAPTER 4

Marketing Strategy – Considerations

Introduction

Before we embark on Section 3, The Marketing Ecosystem, we need to familiarise ourselves with the following marketing concepts:

- Client personas
- Understanding and aligning marketing tactics to the client journey
- Brand marketing vs lead generation marketing
- Acquisition marketing vs retention marketing
- Inbound marketing vs outbound marketing
- Traditional marketing vs digital marketing
- Where science meets creativity
- Marketing vs advertising
- Content marketing

Client personas

In the pre-digital age, businesses generally segmented their potential customers into target audiences based on demographics, eg women over fifty years old living in Sydney. They then created standard messaging and marketing activities that targeted these wide groups of people and reached them via mass-market communications channels such as radio, newspapers and TV shows that serviced that particular group of people.

Modern digital marketing enables you to identify potential clients and communicate with them in a significantly more direct, granular and personalised manner, and hence the concept of client personas was created.

A client persona is an imaginary representation of your ideal client. A firm that offers multiple types of services may have multiple client personas, but it is important to focus on a primary client persona for each service.

Unlike the traditional definition of a target market which was generalised and described demographic characteristics common to many people, eg job title, age, gender, income etc, a client persona is a single fictional character that represents an ideal target customer group, including their key problems, behaviour patterns, psychographics and demographics. It also considers reasons behind why a particular client may behave in a particular way, for example their ambitions, goals, fears etc.

A client persona may include descriptions of actual media consumption by the ideal client. For example, a sports nutritionist may undertake copious amounts of research on the internet, whereas a neurosurgeon may only be guided by accredited university research by highly qualified academic professors and distributed to practitioners through their relevant industry associations.

All your marketing content and messaging should be informed by and communicate directly to your client persona, paying particular attention to their problems. It is, however, important to remember that the client persona is an imaginary character representing a client group. It is not simply a description of one or two (or even three) actual people.

Understanding and aligning marketing tactics to the client journey

There is a common process that most buyers go through leading up to and post purchasing a product or service. It consists of four stages: awareness, consideration, decision and referral.

1. **Awareness stage** – the potential client becomes aware that they have a problem and undertakes research to understand their problem more fully.

2. **Consideration stage** – the potential client understands their problem and is actively researching and comparing alternative solutions.

3. **Decision stage** – the potential client has decided on the service provider and approach they will take to solve their problem.

4. **Referral stage** – although not often considered part of the client journey, this is an important stage in any marketing strategy. The referral stage comes about as a result of the client being so thrilled with you and your solution that they refer you to others.

As a professional legal service provider, you need to help potential clients move through the client journey by providing appropriate communications and content at each stage. Your messaging and content should help educate them on their problems and the solutions to those problems.

As well as delivering relevant content unique to each stage, you can use specific communications channels that are more suited to some stages than others. For example, when a potential client is in the awareness stage, you want to make yourself known to them. You can achieve this in a number of ways, including traditional and digital advertising, SEO, social media and so forth. When clients are in the consideration stage, you will want to engage and educate them using primarily direct communications channels such as email.

High-quality, personal, relevant and timely content engages potential clients and helps them navigate through the client journey to arrive at a decision. When you're developing content for each stage of the client journey, consider its objective, format and subject. It is

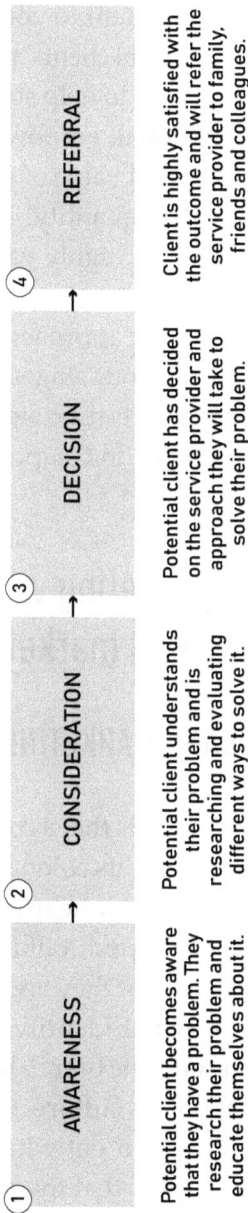

AWARENESS

Potential client becomes aware that they have a problem. They research their problem and educate themselves about it.

CONSIDERATION

Potential client understands their problem and is researching and evaluating different ways to solve it.

DECISION

Potential client has decided on the service provider and approach they will take to solve their problem.

REFERRAL

Client is highly satisfied with the outcome and will refer the service provider to family, friends and colleagues.

Figure 4.1: Client Journey

important to tailor the content to your client personas so that it speaks in your ideal clients' tone and style, and focuses on educating them to help solve their problem. This will be more personal, empower the client and instil trust. The quality and value of your content is far more important than the quantity; it's generally best for content to be short, but highly valuable.

A client-focused marketing approach consists of seven stages, aligning with the four stages of the client journey. The seven stages are discussed in the 7-Step Growth Blueprint detailed in Chapter 7.

Brand marketing vs lead generation marketing

BRAND MARKETING

A common misconception is that a company's brand is its logo and look and feel – its colours, font, letterhead, business cards etc. We often hear graphic designers and other creative marketers talking about having rebranded a company; what they are actually referring to is the company's visual identity (branding). This visual identity represents the brand, but is itself not the brand. A firm's brand is its culture, reputation, values, attributes – the feeling you get when you're dealing with it. A strong analogy is that the brand is the firm's personality, while the branding (logo, look and feel etc) is its face and body.

For example, the heart of Walt Disney's brand is 'Family Magic'. It's a fun, exciting brand, an escape, and all of Walt Disney's movies, products, values and attributes are carefully constructed to reinforce that brand.

Another strong brand is Harley Davidson. Harley Davidson motorcycles represent a highly social, rebellious lifestyle. Riders who subscribe to the Harley Davidson brand display their association through their shared branding – their clothing, and often a Harley Davidson tattoo.

A firm's brand reputation can make or break it. When it comes to medium-sized and small professional services firms, the owner, often without even realising it, creates the brand and brand reputation. Their own personal brand forms the foundations of the business brand.

Your brand is one of your most valuable intellectual assets. It is your reputation and personality, created through your competence, business practices, ethics, values and attributes. When developing your brand, consider your key brand drivers – your strongest and most differentiating attributes and values.

Your brand attributes are the tangible components of your brand, while your brand values reflect the emotional, ethical and philosophical aspects. Words to describe attributes include: family law, personal connection, trust, expertise and premium service. Words to describe values include: client first, make it happen, welcoming, accessible and non-intimidating.

There are some values that are fundamental to the success of all firms, such as honesty, ethics and politeness. These are simply expected by clients, and as such are neither strong nor differentiating.

It is important to remember that the behaviours, attitudes, knowledge and interactions of everyone in the firm reflect the brand. For this reason, once you have defined your attributes and values, ensure everyone in the firm stands by them. In other words, they must live the brand.

Your brand tells people, by way of your actions and behaviours, who and what you are. Once you have articulated your brand, it informs all of your marketing initiatives, including your visual identity.

Brand marketing promotes your brand to potential clients; it does not generally focus on immediate client acquisition. While a strong brand is critical to all businesses, and every firm needs to articulate and live its brand, it is usually only the larger firms that have the financial resources to develop brand advertising.

LEAD GENERATION MARKETING

Lead generation marketing refers to marketing activities specifically designed to initiate potential client enquiries for your services.

Generally, someone becomes a lead when they have shown interest in your services. Leads can be in the awareness, consideration or decision stage of the client journey. A marketing qualified lead (MQL) is a lead who has demonstrated through their behaviours and actions, such as website visits, article downloads, questions they've asked etc, that they are highly engaged and more likely to become a client than other leads.

Two useful metrics for consideration when you're determining the effectiveness of your lead generation activities are cost per lead and cost per client. To calculate cost per lead, simply divide your total marketing cost for a particular lead generation activity by the number of leads generated from that activity. Similarly, by dividing your total marketing cost for a particular lead generation activity by the number of new clients you've generated from that activity, you can calculate its cost per client. You can then compare cost per lead and cost per client metrics across different marketing activities to help inform future lead generation marketing decisions.

While both cost per lead and cost per client are valuable metrics, in isolation they are insufficient to determine the effectiveness of a lead generation activity. You must also consider the total number of leads generated, total number of clients engaged and total lifetime value of the clients from a specific activity. For example, an activity with a high cost per lead may ultimately generate the highest ROI. This could occur where the lead to client conversion rate is higher, or the lifetime value of clients resulting from the activity is higher.

Digital lead generation includes initiatives such as Google advertising, Facebook advertising, SEO, content marketing and webinars etc. Traditional marketing lead generation initiatives include press advertising, radio advertising, events etc.

Acquisition marketing vs retention marketing

The degree of focus you place on acquisition marketing versus retention marketing is based entirely on your business objectives. Whether you skew your marketing activities towards the acquisition of new clients, focus on retaining existing clients, or balance the two will depend on whether your clients have one-time, inter-mittently recurring or regular long-term support needs.

For example, client 1 may be a family man or woman who has just purchased a new property. This client may purchase one or two properties in their lifetime and can be considered a one-time client. Client 2, an intermittently recurring client, may be an investor who purchases a property every few years. Client 3 may be a property developer who is constantly developing and selling properties and has a regular long-term support need.

In situations such as these, you need to determine the effort and budget you will invest in marketing to each type of client. You can base your decision on the revenue and profitability you generate from each client type, as well as your overall business objectives.

The cost of acquiring a new client is substantially higher than the cost of retaining an existing client. Many figures have been suggested as to what the difference in cost is, but in reality, it depends on your business model, channels to market, and the types of services you offer.

There is also a general recognition that long-term clients are more valuable than short-term clients, ie they have a higher lifetime value. While this is often the case, it is not necessarily universal and will depend on each specific situation.

Modern client relationship management (CRM) solutions have simplified the management of new client acquisition and long-term client retention initiatives. An easy-to-implement retention activity could be an automated email campaign that communicates with a previous client every year on the anniversary of their original matter. In the previous example of the property purchase, this email may simply offer relevant and interesting information related to purchasing property. The key is to ensure that the communication is relevant, timely and personalised.

Using modern CRM and marketing automation systems, you can create communications that are personalised and specific to each client. These are more effective and engaging than standard, mass-produced email bulletins or newsletters, as they are more relevant and timely.

Engaging appropriately with clients over the longer term increases not only the likelihood that you will be top of mind when they next need help, but also increases the likelihood of them referring you on to other potential clients.

Inbound marketing vs outbound marketing

INBOUND

Inbound marketing is a relatively new concept made possible by modern technologies. It recognises that technology has changed traditional buying behaviours and that today, the majority of buyers research a service online before even speaking with the service provider.

When a potential client becomes aware that they have a problem, they will then generally conduct online research to better understand their problem. This usually begins with a Google search. Once they understand and can articulate their problem, they search for solutions.

Adopting inbound marketing principles increases the likelihood that a potential client will become aware of your firm during their initial research. Articles and content you have created will appear in their searches and help them understand their problem. Content marketing and SEO are therefore important to ensure that your content appears when the potential client first researches their problem.

As potential clients move through the client journey, they will engage and interact with your content and start recognising you as an expert in the field they require help with. Much of this content is organic, ie it is content on your website, blogs and social media platforms, rather than paid advertising.

When you're creating content to support inbound marketing strategies, your client personas form the basis of the messaging. Your content must be specific and relevant to the people who will be requiring your services, ensuring that it is appropriately structured to attract, engage and nurture potential clients.

OUTBOUND

Unlike inbound marketing, where the potential client finds your valuable content, outbound marketing is predicated on you placing advertising in media such as magazines, newspapers, radio, TV, Facebook, Google and outdoor.

One of the most important differences between inbound and outbound marketing is that inbound marketing is

consumed by qualified buyers, whereas outbound marketing often reaches unqualified audiences. Advertising
on Facebook and Google Display is considered outbound, but these two digital channels do offer a granular targeting approach and reach more qualified buyers
than traditional outbound media.

Outbound marketing is essentially interruption marketing. Your advertisement is distributed far and wide
in the hope that its creative execution will attract the
attention of a potential client. Inbound marketing, on
the other hand, is predicated on qualified buyers finding your useful, educational organic content on the
internet and engaging with your firm as a result. For
this reason, inbound marketing generally engages
prospects with a need for your services.

Effective marketing strategies incorporate elements
of both outbound and inbound marketing. There are
many reasons why a combination of both usually
provides better results than either one alone. While
inbound marketing may sound like every marketer's
dream, in reality, this would not maximise the opportunities available. Being found online through SEO is
a longer-term strategy that you need to complement
with advertising, particularly digital outbound such
as Facebook and Google advertising that can reach a
more precise audience.

For example, Google advertising offers in-market audience targeting. In-market audiences are people Google
has identified as actively researching or comparing

products and services online that are similar to yours. Google takes into account clicks on related ads and subsequent conversions, as well as the content of the sites and pages people visit. It then categorises users so that you can target those most relevant to your advertisement.

Google also offers custom affinity audiences, where you can create an audience for your Google ads based on keywords a person has used in searches, websites they have visited, and places they may be interested in.

Facebook also includes granular targeting options, including a person's interests, job title etc.

Traditional marketing vs digital marketing

We covered traditional and digital marketing extensively in Chapter 3, so let's now move on to...

WHERE SCIENCE MEETS CREATIVITY

Modern marketing is a blend of science, technology and creativity that requires an intellectual and practical understanding of human behaviour. With this understanding, you can use modern technology to deliver relevant communications to the right people at the right time in order to help solve their problems.

No longer is marketing simply based on placing an advertisement in a publication in the hope that someone who sees your advert might be interested enough to respond. Old-school advertising was based on creative executions designed to distract people from what they were doing to make them aware of your existence, whether they had a need for your solution or not. Modern marketing is more scientific, targeted, timely, relevant and measurable. It is about helping people with a need for your solution to find you, and then assisting them with helpful information at the right time and place.

Marketing vs advertising

There is a common misconception among non-marketers that marketing and advertising are one and the same. Advertising is in fact a sub-set of marketing.

Marketing can be thought of as a process that results in solving the problems of potential clients. This process has traditionally incorporated the four Ps:

- Product (service)
- Price
- Promotion (incorporating advertising)
- Place (sales and distribution channels)

Advertising is one form of promotion. It generally takes the form of paid messages that ensure potential clients are aware of the services and solutions you provide. There are, however, many other strategies for making potential clients aware of your services, for example blogging or writing a column for a particular publication.

The difference between marketing and advertising is important to understand because the marketing strategies and tactics to grow your practice that are discussed in this book are first and foremost based on a genuine desire to solve clients' problems. Advertising is merely one tactic in the overall process.

Content marketing

The Content Marketing Institute defines content marketing as 'the marketing technique of creating and distributing relevant and valuable content to attract, engage and acquire a customer'.

A successful content marketing strategy establishes you as a credible expert within your particular field. It demonstrates that you and your firm have a deep understanding of your client's problems and can solve their pain points. Potential clients are naturally inclined to trust those they see as experts and therefore engage your services rather than a competitor's.

Content marketing includes blog posts, eBooks, articles, whitepapers, videos, newsletters, case studies, webinars, infographics etc that are designed to attract, educate and engage potential clients. Content helps to address the questions and concerns of potential clients and move them through the stages of the client journey, from awareness to consideration to decision.

An increase in content marketing has been fuelled by advances in marketing automation and the ease of use of self-publishing tools such as social media, blogs, websites and emailing systems. Interestingly, though, content marketing is not new; it has been practised in print form for many decades. As far back as 1904, Jell-O, a relatively unknown company and product, produced a free recipe book sharing interesting ways to prepare dessert jellies. People realised the value of content marketing when within just two years of releasing the recipe book, Jell-O's sales rose to over $1 million per year.

Some forms of content are better suited to particular stages of the client journey than others. For example:

- **Awareness stage:** content formats can include email, eBooks, video, guides and blogs, and should focus on educating the potential client on the actual problem they have become aware of.

- **Consideration stage:** content formats can include email, videos, whitepapers, and webinars etc, and should focus on the actual solutions to the problems.

- **Decision stage:** content can include email, case studies (where possible), brochures and other collateral, and should focus on the services you provide and your method of solving clients' problems.

- **Referral stage:** content formats include predominantly direct communications such as email and traditional mail.

It is also important to ensure your content is informative and educational (ie it shows you can solve your client's problems). Once you have your content and content plan, you can then consider how best to present it, eg eBook, video, webinar etc.

POPULAR CONTENT MARKETING FORMATS

Video. A video, irrespective of the format (animation, live video, whiteboard style), is easy to watch and digest right through to the end.

Infographics. An infographic is content that is presented in a graphical, visually appealing format, making complex concepts easy to read, understand and remember. They can include colourful diagrams, images, icons etc.

Blog posts. A well-written, relevant blog post will attract attention and is likely to be read through to the end. Blogs are an ideal content format to attract potential clients at the awareness stage of the client journey.

Whitepapers and articles. Whitepapers and articles provide in-depth information on a particular subject and are ideal for potential clients wanting more information than a blog post can provide.

Checklists and guides. Helpful checklists and definitive guides are generally well received as they provide step-by-step processes designed to make the potential client's life easier.

Webinars. Webinars are proving to be one of the most successful content marketing tactics. They feel personal and engaging, and often include a live question and answer session at the end.

Emails. With the growth of marketing automation systems, email is now a critical component of content marketing. Email marketing is relevant across all stages of the client journey and should be personalised, relevant and timely.

| Video | Infographic | Blog | Article |

| Checklist | Webinar | Email |

Figure 4.2: Popular Content Marketing Formats

COPYWRITING

Content marketing needs to be strategic and well executed. Whether the content you create is for a blog post, website page, eBook, or video script, quality copywriting is an important factor in achieving the end result you desire. Copy must be relevant, educational and engaging, and if you're going to use the content on the internet, it should also be search engine optimised.

Finding a good copywriter who can translate complex subjects into easy-to-read marketing copy is essential. They should be familiar with the client journey and associated messaging strategy, email nurture sequences, advertising copy, and SEO copywriting practices. While we can all write copy, good copywriting is a skill best left to the professionals.

Once you have briefed a copywriter, they can research and draft the copy from scratch. Alternatively, you can provide them with a complete draft, which they will polish and fine tune to meet its objectives.

In addition to being an excellent wordsmith, a good copywriter generally follows defined structures and formats appropriate to the type of content they are producing. Most types of content have recognised structures, some of which work better than others. For example, AIDA – attention, interest, desire, action – is a structure commonly adopted by copywriting professionals.

Summary

In this chapter, we have reviewed important consider-ations for when you're developing a marketing strategy. The specific strategies and tactics you employ will be dependent on your firm's overall business objectives.

Considerations include:

- Client personas
- Understanding and aligning marketing tactics to the client journey
- Brand marketing vs lead generation marketing
- Acquisition marketing vs retention marketing
- Inbound marketing vs outbound marketing
- Traditional marketing vs digital marketing
- Where science meets creativity
- Marketing vs advertising
- Content marketing

Before developing a seamlessly aligned marketing strategy, you need to familiarise yourself with the fun-damental marketing concepts that we have covered in this chapter. You may then wish to begin with simple tactical executions, or your firm may be ready to adopt a complete, integrated marketing strategy.

If a person has become aware of a problem that you can help them solve, you need to align your commu-nications with the first three stages of their buying cycle – awareness, consideration and decision. Always design marketing activities with the client journey in mind. By creating strategies and content that engages and helps potential clients at each stage of the client journey, you will naturally draw them to you. In fact, they will often end up engaging your services without you actually doing any selling.

Now that you are familiar with both the framework and concepts of marketing, it is time to look at the marketing ecosystem and the major components that work together to form the ecosystem.

SECTION 3
The Marketing Ecosystem

CHAPTER 5

The Marketing Ecosystem and Owned Media

Introduction

As consumer behaviour and marketing continue to evolve, in order to maximise the benefits and returns from your marketing strategies, you need to consider the various tactics, tools and technologies as an ecosystem.

The term synergy, where the combined effect of the parts is greater than the sum of those parts individually, has never been more applicable to marketing than it is today. Modern marketing is grounded in the fact that many tactics work together to complement each other in a synergistic way that delivers incredible results.

Imagine the world's top eleven soccer players. Individually, not one player would be able to win a game, even against an average team, but put the eleven players together in one team and they would be unbeatable. And so it is with digital marketing. A website on its own achieves little, but combine it with SEO, social media, content marketing, lead magnets, landing pages, blogs, email marketing, advertising and promotions, and marketing automation, and frame it within the client journey, and immediately you have a powerful solution that can drive your firm's growth well into the future.

No longer do individual marketing tactics work in isolation. While one component may be a good start, marketing initiatives require a fully integrated approach to achieve maximum results.

The media components of a marketing ecosystem can be divided into three major categories: owned media, paid media and earned media. I have included a fourth group, all media, which as the name suggests includes media that spans all three categories.

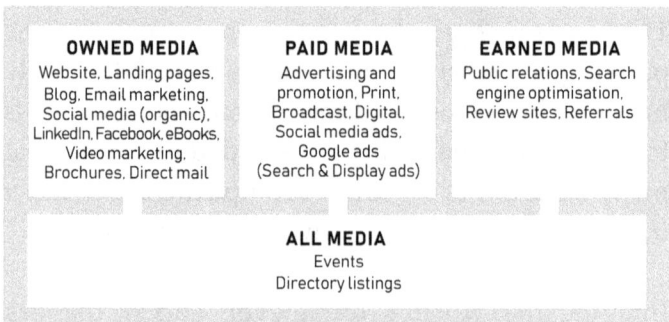

OWNED MEDIA	PAID MEDIA	EARNED MEDIA
Website, Landing pages, Blog, Email marketing, Social media (organic), LinkedIn, Facebook, eBooks, Video marketing, Brochures, Direct mail	Advertising and promotion, Print, Broadcast, Digital, Social media ads, Google ads (Search & Display ads)	Public relations, Search engine optimisation, Review sites, Referrals

ALL MEDIA
Events
Directory listings

Figure 5.1: Owned, Paid, Earned and All Media Types

Due to the extensiveness of owned, paid, earned and all media, I have split the topic across two chapters. This chapter focuses on the power of the marketing ecosystem and owned media, while the following chapter looks at paid, earned and all media types.

The power of the marketing ecosystem

The following example demonstrates the power of the ecosystem. Let's say you've always had a basic website with a 'contact us' page, but no calls to action. It performs as an online brochure that has never been promoted or search engine optimised. Occasionally people stumble across your website, but the majority of visits are from people you've given the website URL to directly. Furthermore, without any analytics tracking, you have no way to know how many daily visits you're getting, where those visitors are coming from, or which pages on the site are most popular.

You've decided it's time to start growing your firm. You provide mediation services and want to add some useful lead magnets to your site. In this case, your lead magnet will simply be a two-page downloadable checklist titled 'The Nine Things You Need To Do Before Engaging A Mediation Lawyer'. In order to download the document, a potential client will simply enter their name and email address, and the checklist will be emailed to them.

On its own, this still won't increase the number of visitors to your site, but at least those who do find your site can download the checklist, and you can capture their name and email address to follow up if and when you have time.

However, let's suppose you now decide to advertise your mediation services to a tightly defined target market based on your client persona, and simultaneously implement a marketing automation solution. The result of these two initiatives alone can significantly increase your website visitors and enable you to automatically communicate, nurture and onboard them as clients, with minimal additional time and effort.

It works as follows:

1. A highly targeted potential client sees your Facebook or Google AdWords advertisement for mediation services.

2. They click on the ad and are taken to a page on your website.

3. The potential client reads the content on the page which provides general information on mediation services.

4. They start to trust your level of expertise and desire further information.

5. There is a call-to-action button on the page that promotes a checklist explaining, for example, the nine things they need to do before engaging a mediation lawyer. They click on the button and are taken to a dedicated landing page where they can request the checklist by completing the form.

6. As they now trust your expertise and legitimacy, they complete the form, entering their name and email address. They are emailed a link to download the checklist.

7. Their details are automatically recorded in your marketing automation system.

8. The marketing system records their interests and behaviours on your website and enters them into a nurturing sequence that sends them additional helpful information at appropriate times, determined by their interests and behaviours.

9. When the potential client reaches a particular stage in the client journey, a message appears on your computer linking you to their entire interaction history, showing the pages they've visited, content they've downloaded, and emails they've engaged with.

10. At this point in time, you can elect to telephone them, or alternatively, the system can automatically send them a personal email from you that includes a link to your appointment scheduling system.

11. Once you have met with the prospect and agreed to proceed, you can automatically email a pre-populated letter of engagement.

The ecosystem I've described above can generate high volumes of leads and nurture them through the awareness, consideration and decision stages of the client journey. Apart from the telephone call or in-person meeting, the entire client engagement process has been facilitated automatically, while you have continued working on other client files.

This is an example of a marketing ecosystem that can deliver massive results with little additional effort from yourself.

What is owned media?

Owned media is any brand exposure where you actually own the media content or channel through which you achieve the exposure. With owned media, you have complete control over how and when it is used.

Owned media includes:

- Website
- Lead magnets
- Landing pages
- Blog
- Email marketing
- Marketing automation
- Social media (organic)
- LinkedIn
- Facebook
- Google My Business
- Video marketing
- Brochures
- Direct mail

WEBSITE

Your website forms the foundation of all your digital marketing activities, and is therefore the central component of your marketing ecosystem. Virtually every initiative integrates with or feeds off your website.

Your website plays an important role at each stage of the client journey, from the potential client becoming aware of you, through to engagement and referral. It does this on a 24/7 basis, 365 days per year. It is, however, important to recognise that simply having a great quality website is no longer sufficient to build a business. There are over a billion websites on the internet. For potential clients to find you, you need your website to be integrated within a solid marketing ecosystem.

Give careful planning and consideration to your website development. It needs to drive the success of your digital marketing activities, which is why the whole of Chapter 8 is devoted to websites.

Lead magnets and landing pages are important elements of a modern website and its associated marketing ecosystem. For this reason, I have referenced them alongside owned media.

LEAD MAGNETS

A lead magnet is valuable content that potential clients can download from your website once they have entered their name and email address in order to do so.

A lead magnet is usually downloadable digital content. However, a lead magnet may be other types of content, such as access to videos, a free consultation, or a webinar etc.

Lead magnets serve five important roles:

- They can be advertised
- They can attract potential clients to your website
- They enable you to learn more about your website visitors and potential clients
- They provide you with the contact details of potential clients
- They enable you to enter potential clients into automated nurturing programs

Once a potential client has requested a lead magnet, you will be able to recognise the problem they need to solve, and hence provide them with the additional information they require as they move through the client journey.

LANDING PAGES

Landing pages are website pages focused on providing visitors with information that helps them address their immediate problem. The most common form of landing page provides some details on a subject and a facility for the visitor to access additional information. The additional information is usually a lead magnet, such as an eBook, that is emailed to them after they complete the request form on the landing page.

Major sections of a landing page include an action-oriented headline, a clearly articulated offer, a form, and minimal external navigation.

It is standard practice to link online advertisements to a landing page, rather than a homepage or general website page, because the landing page is dedicated to the content in the advertisement. By clicking on the advert, visitors are taken directly to the content they are interested in, rather than being forced to wade through copious amounts of website content that could be irrelevant to their needs.

Make sure your landing page and lead magnets are of high perceived value to the visitor, demonstrate your knowledge, and help the visitor solve at least one of their problems.

BLOG

A blog, in the context of law firm marketing, is a webpage that is regularly updated with new content related to your firm and the legal industry. The content is structured in article format, with a main blog page listing all of the articles or article categories. Once your visitor clicks on any particular article, it will open for them to read in a page of its own.

Blogs can help attract potential clients to your website, position you as an expert, and improve SEO.

Each blog article should be search engine optimised around a particular topic, so that when a potential client does a Google search on that topic, your article will appear. Your blog article should include links to content on your website, as well as call-to-action buttons that link to landing pages from which visitors can access lead magnets. The lead magnets should provide additional information that expands on the blog article.

Additionally, it is good practice to include social media sharing links in the blog post to allow readers to share your content and increase its exposure.

EMAIL MARKETING

Email marketing has traditionally been poorly executed by many businesses, which has led to a perception that all email marketing is simply old-school spam. This is not correct. Email marketing has advanced considerably since the early days of basic email newsletter distribution. Used in the correct context, professional, client-centric email marketing is one of the most valuable resources for both potential clients and law firms. It involves sending the right emails to the right audience at the right time; it is absolutely not about purchasing lists and randomly spamming people's email inboxes.

Unlike traditional emails and newsletters, which were often spam, today's email strategies engage and nurture recipients who have already shown interest in your firm in some way. For example, they may have downloaded content from your website or be an existing client.

Modern marketing techniques ensure email communications are timely, relevant and personalised. By adopting these three principles, you will remain top of clients' and prospects' minds, and they will look forward to your emails. Irrespective of whether you are communicating with one, 100 or even 1,000 clients and potential clients, modern email marketing allows you to automatically customise and personalise each individual email to each recipient.

Appropriate list segmentation is important to ensure emails are timely, relevant and personalised. An email for a potential client who is still in the early stages of awareness will communicate a different message from an email to a potential client in the consideration or decision-making stage. When you combine email marketing with marketing automation, you can distribute literally hundreds of thousands of personalised emails addressing each specific recipient's needs. Email is ideally suited to nurturing leads into becoming clients.

For example, let's say someone has spent a considerable amount of time on your website, browsing content related to injuries sustained in a motor vehicle accident. They have also downloaded content that further confirms their interest in this subject. Using intelligent email marketing, you can automatically send the potential client additional relevant information that is not freely available on your website.

Highly personalised automated email marketing is not about sending a standard monthly newsletter to clients and prospective clients. By identifying a potential client's problems via their behaviours and the answers they have entered into your online forms, you can send personalised, relevant and helpful communications to the right people at the right time.

Ensuring the emails are timely, relevant, and personalised requires you to identify where the prospective client is in their client journey, and lead them through the journey with additional content. For a potential client in the awareness stage, emails that provide links to videos, guides and eBooks that educate them on their problems are very valuable, whilst potential clients in the consideration stage will benefit from emails that provide links to FAQ sheets, videos, webinars, eBooks and articles that address solutions to their problems. Webinars can be pre-recorded and made available to the right people at the right time. When a potential client reaches the decision stage, they are likely to find an invitation to a free initial consultation most useful.

Emails can include links
to any of the following

(1) AWARENESS	(2) CONSIDERATION	(3) DECISION	(4) REFERRAL

EDUCATIONAL CONTENT ABOUT ISSUE/PROBLEM

eBooks
Guides
Videos
Blogs

EDUCATIONAL CONTENT ON VARIOUS SOLUTIONS

Videos
Articles
Whitepapers
eBooks
FAQ sheets
Webinars

FOCUS ON ONBOARDING POTENTIAL CLIENT

Invitation to free consultation
Case studies
Brochures

REGULAR ONGOING COMMUNICATIONS

Newsletters
Birthday cards
End of year greetings

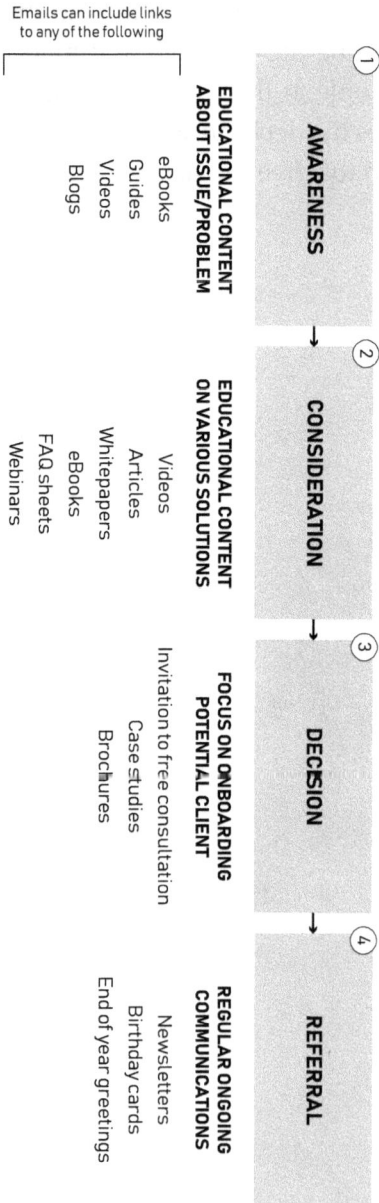

Figure 5.2: Email Content by Client Journey Stage

Email marketing helps the potential client move through the client journey to a point where they feel comfortable and ready to meet with you. Too often, though, firms lead with the free consultation. In reality, this strategy is putting the cart before the horse, as the client needs to be ready to engage with your firm when you offer the free consultation.

It may take a series of emails to build trust and earn a client's business. This is called lead nurturing, and it is the process of developing a relationship with a potential client, the objective being to win their business when they are ready to engage. You may be thinking this sounds like an overwhelming task that you simply don't have time for. In reality, email marketing and lead nurturing can be easily and cost-effectively automated. Once you have set up the process, potential clients will receive timely, relevant and personalised communications from you with limited additional demands on your time.

MARKETING AUTOMATION

Marketing automation is a critical component of a successful digital marketing ecosystem. Marketing automation systems offer extensive functionality designed to manage lead acquisition, maximise lead conversions, nurture potential clients, and increase repeat business and referrals.

Chapter 9 explains the major benefits of such a system,

but at its most fundamental level, a marketing automation system enables you to automatically communicate with potential and existing clients, based on the behaviours and actions that they take on your website and in response to your communications.

Marketing automation systems such as KEAP/Infusionsoft, HubSpot, Active Campaign and ONTRAPORT incorporate their own unified CRM functionality that allows you to segment the database, personalise communications and send content to the right people at exactly the right time.

In addition to client acquisition and nurturing, marketing automation systems can also streamline internal operational processes, making your firm more efficient. For example, it is often possible to automatically distribute relevant documents to clients at the appropriate times by integrating with document management systems such as DocuSign and PandaDoc.

SOCIAL MEDIA (ORGANIC)

Organic social media provides a wonderful opportunity to position yourself as an authority in your area of expertise without incurring advertising fees or charges. An organic post is a free post on your social media profiles, for example on your personal Facebook feed, your business Facebook page, your LinkedIn profile, or your Twitter feed.

There are different ways you can leverage these free posts. For example, an effective strategy is to write a blog post for your website, and then leverage it by linking to it from your social media accounts.

Over the past few years, Facebook has significantly restricted the number of people who will see your organic business page posts. However, there is an option to boost posts for a small fee and have them seen by a greater audience.

Once potential clients have seen your post, they click through to your website, read the blog, and then respond to a call to action in your blog to either download or access additional information (lead magnet). Once they have requested the lead magnet, you are able to identify their immediate interests and communicate with them in a meaningful and useful way, using the email marketing strategies we discussed previously.

In addition to posts and links to blog articles, there are numerous other organic social media opportunities, such as:

- Facebook Live (ability to livestream video to anyone who wishes to join in).
- The ability to post short ideas, messages or video on your Facebook profile feeds.
- The ability to post short ideas, messages or video on your LinkedIn profile feeds.

- The ability to draft longer articles within the LinkedIn platform itself and post them to relevant LinkedIn groups that you are a member of. These articles are similar to blogs on your website, but are contained within the LinkedIn platform. Most groups welcome useful content, but generally don't allow promotional articles and posts.

- All posts and articles need to be useful and educational in nature, rather than sales focused. Educational posts help position you as an authority, and as such draw interest and leads, despite being non-sales focused in nature.

A 2018 Sensis social media survey showed that 64% of consumers are more likely to trust a brand if it interacts positively on social media.[12] Research of 1,000 Australian small and medium-sized businesses (SMEs) found that social media was being used by almost half of SMEs and by 60% of larger businesses. Over 16 million Australians are now on social media.

Social media helps you amplify your content and engage positively with more potential and existing clients by giving your firm personality and accessibility. There are numerous social media channels available, for example LinkedIn, Facebook, Twitter, Instagram, YouTube, WeChat, Tumblr, Pinterest and many more. The key social media channels that best serve the interests of advocacy lawyers are Facebook and LinkedIn.

---

12. www.sensis.com.au/about/our-reports/sensis-social-media -report

Other useful channels to consider are YouTube and Twitter.

LINKEDIN

While Facebook is the largest social media platform, LinkedIn can be the more appropriate channel to develop your authority and positioning among professional business people.

Developing an active LinkedIn profile through drafting and posting regular content, such as articles, images and videos, participating in group discussions, and even advertising on the LinkedIn platform helps to increase your exposure, position you as an expert, and enable you to interact with other professionals.

FACEBOOK

Facebook offers a range of marketing opportunities, including advertising, private groups, direct messaging, and company pages.

A Facebook business page is a business profile you can create for your firm. While a Facebook business page provides exposure and the ability to interact and communicate with existing and potential clients, it also offers many 'insights' that can help support and direct your marketing efforts. For example, Facebook Insights provides data that can help you better understand your client profile.

With a Facebook business page, you can create and invite people to events, receive client reviews, showcase your services, enable clients to send private messages to your firm, and invite them to connect with you via your page. Once you have created your page, you can start a Facebook advertising account for your firm. We will cover Facebook advertising in the 'Paid media' section of Chapter 6.

Facebook also provides analytics on each of your posts, such as your post engagement, reach, likes, comments and shares, which all helps you to measure, analyse and improve your marketing and client acquisition rates.

GOOGLE MY BUSINESS

A Google My Business listing is one of the first places to be when you're embarking on a listing strategy. Apart from the many advantages of a directory listing, a Google My Business listing can increase the likelihood of your business appearing in Google Maps and Google searches.

Google My Business has many advanced features to help increase your firm's exposure. In addition to standard business information such as name, address, operating hours etc, Google My Business also includes posts, reviews, photos, videos and advertisements. Google My

Business advertisements are created through AdWords Express, which helps potential clients discover your business through ads on Google Search as well as Google Maps. When potential clients in your vicinity search for your type of service, your ads may appear next to their search results, along with your contact details.

VIDEO MARKETING

Video marketing has grown exponentially over the last few years. According to HubSpot, 78% of people watch online videos every week,[13] and Cisco believes that by 2020, online videos will make up more than 80% of all consumer internet traffic.[14] HubSpot has also suggested that 55% of people pay close attention to videos, more than any other content type.[15]

Video is not restricted to advertisements. Because a video is significantly more engaging than static images, it can be used to better engage with potential clients browsing your website. When it's personal, a video builds trust, and is also easy to view and share on mobile devices.

---

13. https://biteable.com/blog/tips/video-marketing-statistics
    https://blog.hubspot.com/marketing/video-marketing
14. https://biteable.com/blog/tips/video-marketing-statistics
    https://cisco.com/c/en/us/solutions/collateral/service-provider
    /visual-networking-index-vni/white-paper-c11-741490.html
15. https://biteable.com/blog/tips/video-marketing-statistics

There are different types of video production, from costly high-end productions requiring professional equipment and operators, through to low-cost self-filmed videos where you simply present to a mobile phone. Other types include animated explainer videos, whiteboard animations and, more recently, videos created from still images. Interestingly, self-filmed videos are frequently the most personal, engaging and trust building.

There is no longer an expectation that all videos must be high cost and have high-end production value. Depending on your firm's brand positioning and objectives, you may decide a highly polished video fits best with your strategy. Alternatively, a low-cost personal and engaging video may meet your needs better.

BROCHURES

A major benefit of a brochure is that it makes an intangible service tangible. And if your potential clients are able to touch and feel something, it evokes a sense of confidence in your service. Brochures can also be handed to potential clients, ensuring they have the information they need at their fingertips without having to access it online. Unlike digital media, it remains easily accessible and visible and doesn't disappear once something else is displayed on the screen.

Brochures come in many different shapes, sizes, formats and quality, and can be used to address many objectives. However, all brochures should follow a defined format.

Once you are clear on the objective and audience for your brochure, you need to design the front cover and back page to attract attention and be impactful. In essence, they should resonate with your potential client and evoke an emotional response.

Internal pages begin by articulating your potential clients' problem, your solutions, and the benefits of your particular solutions. They then show proof of how your solutions have benefited previous clients (within any relevant legal and association guidelines), and finally include a compelling call to action.

The call to action moves the prospect from their current position in the client journey to the next stage, generally the awareness to the consideration stage, although it can also be from the consideration to the decision stage. The call to action needs to compel the potential client to behave in the way you want them to, such as contacting your firm, scheduling an appointment or requesting additional information.

DIRECT MAIL

Direct mail consists of any physical promotional item mailed to someone via a traditional postal or courier service. It is usually a printed item such as a flyer, brochure or catalogue.

With the advent of email and the associated lower costs to produce and fulfil messaging online, there has been a noticeable reduction in the use of direct mail in recent years. However, smart marketers have taken advantage of this reduction and are starting to use direct mail again to cut through the email clutter and resonate with ideal prospects. For example, you may decide to send a direct mail piece to a potential client in the awareness or consideration stage who has downloaded an eBook or other item online and has met various qualification requirements.

While direct mail costs are relatively high, the ROI often justifies incorporating it as part of an integrated marketing strategy. With digital printing, it is now possible to print on-demand direct mail as and when required.

Summary

The marketing ecosystem comprises four high-level media categories – owned, paid, earned and all – and each category has a number of media types within it. While you can use an individual media type in isolation, it is when all of these categories and tactics work together and leverage off each other that your business can achieve the greatest growth results.

Owned media types include:

- Website
- Lead magnets

- Landing pages
- Blog
- Email marketing
- Marketing automation
- Social media (organic)
- LinkedIn
- Facebook
- Google My Business
- Video marketing
- Brochures
- Direct mail

In this chapter, we have reviewed owned media. In the next chapter, we will look at paid, earned and all media categories.

CHAPTER 6

Paid, Earned and All Media

Introduction

Following on from our review of owned media in Chapter 5, we now review paid, earned and all media categories.

Paid media types include:

- Print advertising
- Broadcast advertising
- Digital advertising

Earned media types include:

- Public relations exposure
- Search engine optimisation
- Review sites
- Referrals

All media types include:

- Events
- Online directory listings

Paid media

Paid media is any media that requires you to pay a third party to receive advertising exposure, eg newspapers, TV, Facebook, Google advertising. While you maintain a degree of control over paid media, eg you can turn your advertising on and off as desired, it offers less control than you have with owned media.

Advertising and promotions are ideally suited to attracting people in the first stage of the client journey, the awareness stage. Once aware of your firm, they then make contact, either online or offline.

There are three main categories of paid media relevant to medium and smaller-sized law firms that you can incorporate into your marketing and advertising strategy, depending on your firm's business objectives. These are print, broadcast and digital media.

PRINT ADVERTISING

Print advertisements are printed on a physical material, generally paper. Magazines, newspapers, outdoor signs, postcards, direct mail etc are all examples of print advertising media.

Newspaper advertising is one of the more popular types of print advertising and warrants a little further discussion. There are many different types of newspapers that you can consider for your advertising, from exposure in daily national press to local coverage in community newspapers.

Distribution of daily newspapers has declined considerably over the last ten years, as more readers move to online news consumption. However, local newspapers can be a good option if you run a law firm and are looking to grow in your local area. These newspapers help engender community spirit and connection, which tends to increase trust. People like to feel connected, and community newspapers help achieve this feeling.

Similar to daily newspapers, community newspapers are embracing the digital age and many can now be found in both print and online versions. In addition to standard advertising, many newspapers, particularly community based newspapers, also offer editorial coverage.

BROADCAST ADVERTISING

Broadcast is a traditional form of mass-market media that includes TV, radio and cinema advertising etc. While this media has traditionally been costly in urban and city areas, it is more affordable in smaller towns and country areas.

DIGITAL ADVERTISING

Digital advertising generally refers to advertising on social media, search engines and website display advertising.

Social media (Facebook)[16]

Social media advertising refers to paid ads on social media platforms such as Facebook and LinkedIn. These come in many different formats and offer highly granular audience targeting. Social media ads generally link back to landing pages on your website.

Social media advertising has become one of the most popular forms of advertising. Once your firm has a social media profile page, you are able to execute numerous different advertising and promotional strategies.

Facebook is an incredibly powerful advertising solution that can be effective at all stages of the client journey. There are various advertising formats, from single image and text, through to carousel (numerous images) and video ads. I will now outline some of the features that make Facebook advertising so powerful.

---

16. www.facebook.com/business

You have the ability to target potential clients at various stages of the client journey. Facebook refers to these stages as awareness, consideration, and conversion (decision). At the awareness stage, the various ad types help generate awareness of your firm and your services. At the consideration stage, the advertising options help get potential clients thinking about your firm and looking for more information about it. Conversion stage options encourage potential clients who are interested in your business to engage your services. You also have the ability to A/B test your ads, ie create multiple versions of your ads and test which versions perform best.

You can target ads to potential clients based on numerous criteria, including:

- Core audiences, which include factors such as age, gender, location and interests (industry, hobbies, relationships, job titles etc)

- Custom audiences enable you to advertise to existing clients, known prospects, and people who have previously visited your website

- Lookalike audiences allow you to use your existing client information to advertise to others with similar characteristics and interests

You can schedule your ads to run at specific times and days only, as well as define daily or total campaign budgets. Facebook also provides sophisticated analytics, conversion reporting and insights, which all help increase your advertising success.

The following example illustrates the power of Facebook advertising. Let's say you offer conveyancing services. Using your client list, you can advertise to people who share similar characteristics and behaviours to your existing clients, and are therefore likely to require your support and services.

The power of Facebook advertising can present incredible opportunities to law firms.

Google Ads[17]

Google offers different types of advertisements, some of which allow you to target specific audiences, while others are not aimed at any particular audience, but will appear to anyone using a particular keyword in a Google search.

Google's advertising options include: search ads, display ads, shopping ads, video ads on YouTube, and in-app ads. For the purpose of law firm marketing, we will focus on search and display ads.

Google Search ads. Search ads are text-based ads presented to potential clients on the Google search results page when they are looking for information on the services you offer. They can be targeted to potential clients in certain countries, regions, cities, or within a fixed distance from a stipulated location.

---

17. https://ads.google.com/intl/en_au/home

Search ads appear above and below the organic search results. They are triggered by keywords or phrases that you specify. Once you have created the text content for your ads and specified the trigger keywords, you set a budget.

When someone clicks on your ad, they are taken to a page that you stipulate in the ad, generally a unique landing page on your website exclusively related to the content of the ad.

Google Display ads. Digital display ads include the image- and video-based advertisements people see when browsing websites. There are many audience targeting options available, and you can define at a granular level whom each advert will be presented to.

Google Display ads are most commonly image-based ads that can appear on various websites across the internet, and even within Gmail accounts. The Google Display advertising network includes over 2 million different websites on which your ads can be displayed. The main types of display ads to consider within your law firm marketing strategy include:

- Text display ads, which are similar to the ads on Google Search. They can include a headline, two lines of text and a URL link.

- Google Display banner ads, which can display static images or rich media such as video. These ads are available in various sizes and layouts, and can include interactive elements, animations, and more.

- Gmail ads, which appear in someone's Gmail inbox. The recipient can view, save or forward your ad from their inbox.

Display ads can be set up to target specific audiences. Some of the more popular targeting options relevant to law firms include remarketing, custom affinity and in-market audiences.

Remarketing ads are shown to people who have visited your website, or specific pages on your website, as they browse the internet. These ads remind them of your services and help nurture them. Custom affinity ads allow you to define the audiences you want your ad to be presented to, based on their interests and the previous websites they've visited. In-market audiences are potential clients who are in the market, ie currently researching services that you offer, and are considering engaging with a provider.

Google advertising can be very powerful, and is one of the only forms of advertising that will specifically target people looking for your services. Like Facebook, Google provides performance statistics and insights that allow you to measure, review and modify your ads where necessary.

Earned media

This is unpaid exposure through third party media that you have earned, but have no direct control over, for example customers sharing your content on social media, PR exposure, Google ranking you on its SERP, etc.

PUBLIC RELATIONS EXPOSURE (PR)

PR activities relate to the distribution of information between you (or your firm) and the public. This is achieved by creating topics of interest that media outlets believe is valuable and worthy of sharing. As you do not pay for PR exposure, the content you wish to distribute must be highly newsworthy.

PR's ultimate objectives are to inform potential clients of your existence and expertise, create a positive perception of you and your firm, and let them know that you can solve their problem when the need arises. However, unlike an ad, PR achieves this via association rather than direct announcement. An example of a newsworthy story might be that you have been asked to handle the affairs of a high-profile celebrity.

SEARCH ENGINE OPTIMISATION (AN INTRODUCTION)

A website that cannot be found by potential clients is like having an advertising billboard in the middle of the desert. It is of no value to anyone.

SEO is the process of optimising your website pages and executing various actions on them so that they rank highly on a search engine's results page when a potential client undertakes a search related to your firm's services. The purpose is to ensure more people are exposed to your firm. SEO is therefore an important component of the first stage of the client journey, when a potential client becomes aware of their problem.

While addressing SEO is fundamental for any firm wishing to grow, it is a long-term strategy. Over time, SEO can become one of your most valuable lead generation strategies, but it is just one tactic in the marketing ecosystem. Complementing your SEO initiatives with search advertising (pay per click), social media advertising, content marketing, and other lead generation activities is imperative.

We will cover SEO in detail in Chapter 8.

REVIEW SITES

It's often said that your best salespeople are not your employees, but your customers. This is because a growing number of people now rely on and trust online reviews and recommendations more than the advice of a salesperson.

Most credible online directories provide the ability for clients to leave reviews. These include Google, Facebook, and more specifically for Australian firms, TrueLocal.

While it is not always appropriate for clients to leave reviews, particularly where their matters are sensitive or they need to remain anonymous, there are instances where a review may be appropriate. For example, conveyancing cases may generally be less sensitive.

Most clients are happy to leave reviews, so include a request for a review in your emails once the client's matter is positively concluded. Make sure you provide a link to your preferred review site.

REFERRALS

Although law firms can no longer rely on them entirely, referrals are an invaluable part of the marketing ecosystem. Of course, you have no control whatsoever over whether or not your clients will refer your services to friends and family, but if you have followed the approaches described in this book and your marketing is professional, ethical, and focused on helping the client solve their problems, there is a high chance that they will respond favourably with positive reviews and referrals.

All media

Some media types can span all three of the categories we have discussed. For example, an event can be your own (owned), paid (you've paid to participate in someone else's event), or earned (you've been invited to participate in someone else's event at no cost – or you may even be paid to participate in it).

EVENTS

Events include both physical (live on-site) and online initiatives such as conferences, seminars, webinars and talks. Event participation is an excellent way to position yourself as a leader in your field. Speaking at events helps you to increase the awareness of yourself and your firm, and maximises your credibility. In addition to your actual presentation, you can also promote your attendance at the event through advertising and client communications, which will further increase your profile.

Industry commentators frequently attend and report on events. Through their online and printed publications, they can broadcast your message to a wide external audience. Industry events often result in new personal connections, which help with lead generation and client acquisition. There may be opportunities for you to include promotional materials such as brochures and other items in each delegate's conference pack. However, you need to use speaking opportunities to share your knowledge and help educate delegates, as opposed to hard selling.

Events to consider speaking at include legal industry-specific events, your target market industry events, and even client-organised conferences and events, particularly if you are working with larger businesses. It is, however, important to remember that the type of events you attend must relate back to your overall business objectives.

ONLINE DIRECTORY LISTINGS

Directories have always been an important component of marketing, right back to the early days of printed business directories such as the *Yellow Pages*. Today, though, online directories play an even greater importance in that they help improve the SEO of your website and rank your listings in Google searches.

There are numerous directories that you can list your firm on, but not all directories are equal. While some will add value and credence to your website and SEO, others can actually harm your search rankings. It's therefore important to ensure you only list in credible directories that support your SEO efforts. Good examples include local business directories and Google My Business.

As much as possible, ensure that your directory listings include comprehensive descriptions, contact details and images. Many directories also include a review section where clients can leave reviews. Positive client reviews are extremely powerful for attracting potential clients in the decision stage.

Summary

Modern marketing tactics are a menu of options from which you can select the most appropriate to achieve your particular business objectives. Use each tactic strategically to support your potential client's stage in the client journey. You achieve the greatest results when you use the appropriate tactics in a way that enables them to leverage off each other.

In this chapter, we have reviewed paid, earned and all media types.

Paid media types include:

- Print advertising
- Broadcast advertising
- Digital advertising

Earned media types include:

- Public relations exposure
- Search engine optimisation
- Review sites
- Referrals

All media types include:

- Events
- Online directory listings

We are now ready to move on to the final stage of the marketing plan, the execution.

Executing a Modern Marketing Plan

CHAPTER 7

The 7-Step Growth Blueprint

Introduction

Understanding the various components and interactions of the marketing ecosystem can feel overwhelming. One would be excused for wondering where to start, or even how it all comes together. Fortunately, there are proven processes that break it down into simple steps, making it easy to design and implement a solid marketing strategy.

You will recall from earlier chapters that the client journey comprises of four stages that potential clients move through on their way to selecting and recommending a service provider. These stages are awareness, consideration, decision and referral. The 7-Step Growth Blueprint provides a strategic framework that helps potential clients move through the four stages of the client journey, engage with your firm and recommend you to others. It includes the following seven steps: attract, trust, engage, nurture, onboard, impress and loyalty. Each stage of the client journey relates to one or more stages in the 7-Step Growth Blueprint.

Let's now look at how the 7-Step Growth Blueprint complements the client journey and maximises the growth of your firm.

The client journey

There are three stages in the client journey leading up to a potential client's decision to engage your services, and a fourth stage that is important once the client has engaged with you and is using your services. The first three stages are awareness, consideration and decision, and the fourth stage is referral.

STAGE 1 – AWARENESS

At the awareness stage, a potential client has become aware of a problem. They don't fully understand their problem, and therefore begin researching it. A problem could be an opportunity, need, or simply a desire for something – anything that causes them to research a subject with the need to solve an issue.

As an example, imagine someone is purchasing a new house. In the awareness stage, they realise they will need to submit documentation, but they don't know exactly what documentation they'll require. They may be asking themselves, 'What documentation requirements will I need to comply with when I purchase my new house next month?'

The person would then start researching the documentation required for the purchase of a new house. They may ask family, friends or colleagues, but they will almost certainly do their own online research.

STAGE 2 – CONSIDERATION

In the consideration stage, a potential client understands their problem, they are undertaking extensive research on solutions, and are considering the alternatives for addressing and solving their issue.

They are aware that you, as a lawyer, could solve some of their problems, but potentially other lawyers could too. Potential clients are, therefore, weighing up your solutions versus other solutions in order to make a decision that will be best for them.

In the example above, the potential client is now aware of the paperwork they require for the purchase of their new property. They are aware that they need to seek the services of conveyancers, lawyers, bank representatives, finance brokers, building inspectors etc, and they are considering the advantages and disadvantages of various providers for each type of service.

Once they know the advantages and disadvantages of each service provider, they can then move to the decision stage.

STAGE 3 – DECISION

At the decision stage, the potential client is ready to commit. They may, however, still not be entirely sure whether they should engage a conveyancer or lawyer, and may need clarification or an incentive to help with their final decision. At this stage, you may offer them an initial thirty-minute consultation at no charge, which is an incentive that may ultimately result in them engaging your firm to provide the services.

STAGE 4 – REFERRAL

Once you have been selected as the client's preferred supplier, the referral stage follows your engagement.

It is well known that winning new clients is significantly more costly than retaining existing clients. A loyalty program increases the chances of your client not only returning to you, but also referring your services on to family, friends and colleagues.

While your service for a particular client may be a one-time service, it is highly likely that the client will be connected with others who will require similar support and representation. By delighting your client, you will ensure that you will be referred on to their family, friends and connections. Additionally, your firm may offer other services that your client requires, such as support setting up a new business or providing mediation services.

Maintaining an ongoing relationship with past clients is easier and cheaper than ever before. You may simply set up an automatically generated email wishing them a happy birthday each year. Alternatively, depending on the service you provided, you may update them on a regular basis with information relevant to that service. Modern technology allows you to delight your clients with minimal time or investment on your part.

Introducing the 7-Step Growth Blueprint

The 7-Step Growth Blueprint provides a strategic framework that helps potential clients move through the four stages of the client journey. It forms the foundation on which your marketing strategy is developed and helps position you and your firm as the most credible authority in your area of expertise. By engaging with potential clients early in their client journey, you are already well positioned to become their provider of choice. The seven steps in the Growth Blueprint are attract, trust, engage, nurture, onboard, impress and loyalty.

Figure 7.1: 7-Step Growth Blueprint

Each step aligns with the client journey as follows:

STAGES OF THE 7-STEP GROWTH BLUEPRINT	STAGES OF THE CLIENT JOURNEY
Attract	Awareness
Trust	Consideration (early stage)
Engage	Consideration (mid-stage)
Nurture	Consideration (late-stage)
Onboard	Decision
Impress	Referral
Loyalty	Referral

STEP 1 – ATTRACT

With the majority of potential clients now referring to the internet before they even contact a service provider, it is virtually guaranteed that they will undertake a Google search as one of the first steps in researching their problem. At this stage in a potential client's journey, they need to become aware of your presence, so you must be easy to find. Your advertising and content should relate directly to the problem the client has become aware of.

As they have only recently become aware of their problem, they may not yet be ready to commit to any supplier without further research. For this reason a sales pitch or incentive offer would be premature, and the potential client may even perceive it as an inappropriate hard-sales tactic.

People buy from people they know, like and trust. At this stage, the potential client knows very little about you and your firm. They have not yet formed a liking or dislike for you. This first stage of the Growth Blueprint is, therefore, all about helping potential clients become aware of you.

Your acquisition and lead generation activities are critical at this early stage. They can include:

SEO

When a potential client conducts a Google search related to the issue they need solving, a solid, ongoing SEO strategy will help your firm's website and other useful content appear high up in the organic results page. Potential clients will then easily be able to see your website description and click on your listing, which takes them to either a specific landing page on your website, or your home page.

Google Search advertising

When the potential client conducts their search, in addition to your organic SEO listing, your firm's Google Search advertisement will feature prominently on the results page. The advertisement will be positioned towards either the top or the bottom of the page, and should link back to a dedicated landing page on your website.

Google Display advertising

This enables you to place image ads on websites in the Google Display network. These ads can take various forms, such as images, video etc, and link back to your website. There are a number of different targeting options, particularly Google's custom affinity and in-market options, that you need to consider when creating advertising strategies.

Facebook advertising

Depending on the services you offer, Facebook advertising may be an effective and appropriate form of promotion. With Facebook advertising, it is possible to target specific groups of people based on factors such as their interests, job titles and demographic profiles. It is also possible to create custom audiences, such as lookalike audiences who share similar characteristics to your existing client base.

Social media strategy

A social media strategy includes paid advertising and organic posts, both of which should lead to valuable content from which the potential client can reach more detailed information. The major social media platforms all provide advertising and organic content opportunities.

Traditional advertising

Traditional forms of advertising, such as newspapers, flyers and radio, can be effective in generating potential client visits to your website, where you can then start the engagement process.

STEP 2 – TRUST

Step 2, trust, aligns with the early part of the consideration stage of the client journey. Once a potential client has seen your advertisement or search engine results listing, you then need to ensure you help them get to know, like and trust you.

Until potential clients have had the chance to get to know, like and trust you or your firm, they will generally be uncomfortable providing their name and contact details to you. For this reason, it is still somewhat premature to require them to provide such details in order to download content.

A more appropriate strategy is to provide some limited but quality information without requiring them to provide any details or complete a form. This information will start building familiarity and is the first step in the potential client liking and trusting you. It is also the first step in establishing yourself as an authority and expert on the subject matter relevant to them.

Your advertising, promotions and content will attract potential clients' attention by relating to their problems. Once they have engaged with your freely provided content, they will be more comfortable providing their details (usually name and email address) to access more in-depth content that will help answer further questions they may have.

The type of content that is ideal in the trust stage includes thought leadership content, tips, checklists, FAQs, and diagnostic scorecards (ie a scorecard that determines, based on the potential client's responses, whether they would benefit from your services). It is important that each initial content piece includes a call to action that leads to more detailed information which requires the potential client's name and email address to access.

You can deliver free initial content through channels such as blogs, YouTube, social media and website pages.

Blogging

Blogs that educate, inform and complement your SEO strategies are often listed on Google Search results pages when a potential client undertakes a relevant search. Additionally, your blogs may be referenced on other websites, which are then also returned in Google Searches, delivering even more visibility and credibility to your firm.

Towards both the middle and end of each blog, include an appropriate call-to-action button that leads to further in-depth content (a lead magnet). Once on the lead magnet's landing page, the potential client is required to fill in a form, entering their name and email address to access the additional content.

YouTube videos

If you create a YouTube channel that links to your website and correctly tags videos, your videos may also be indexed in the Google Search results page. Videos are excellent for generating engagement because they are easy for prospects to consume and therefore highly likely to be watched.

Videos can be hosted on YouTube and displayed on your website. Once a potential client has viewed the video, make sure you direct them to an appropriate call-to-action and lead magnet.

Social media

Like blogging, organic posts, whether they're on LinkedIn, Facebook or other social media, increase awareness and position you as an expert. LinkedIn, for example, enables you to draft articles within its platform and share them easily with your connections and any LinkedIn groups you have joined.

Website pages

Website pages need to provide enough content to encourage potential clients to like and trust you, but access to additional detailed information will require them to provide their name and email address.

Once the potential client arrives at your free content page from an ad or external listing, make sure the content you present is consistent and directly related to what they have just seen in the advertisement. For example, if they have clicked on an ad referencing divorce law, they must be taken to a blog or website landing page specifically related to divorce law. They should not be taken to a generic homepage.

STEP 3 – ENGAGE

The engage step aligns with the middle of the consideration stage of the client journey. It refers to the potential client accessing more detailed content after consuming the free content in the trust stage. They do this by providing their name and email address on a short form. The form can be placed either at the end or alongside the free content, or it can be placed on a separate landing page accessed via a call-to-action button within or alongside the free content.

While eBooks are common lead magnets, there are a number of other types of lead magnets that offer benefits to a potential client for which they may be happy to provide their details. These could include guides, checklists, webinars, videos, FAQ sheets etc.

STEP 4 – NURTURE

Once the potential client has provided their contact details and downloaded the additional information you offered in step 3 (engage), you can start nurturing them. In the nurture phase, you proactively provide them with additional information to help them make their final decision.

The nurture stage provides you with an opportunity to answer any questions that your potential clients may still have after reading or consuming your initial content. During this stage, you build a relationship with them with the intention of earning their business when they are ready.

The potential client has now become a real prospect. Nurturing utilises predominantly one-to-one communications such as an email drip campaign (a series of relevant, personalised and timely communications) to form a deeper relationship between your firm and the prospect, rather than external promotion such as SEO, Facebook, Google etc.

Although nurturing requires you to form a direct relationship between yourself and your prospect, it does not necessarily require any additional time or involvement on your part. Marketing automation systems (which we discuss in detail in Chapter 9) are designed to automate drip communications at each stage of the 7-Step Growth Blueprint. Virtually the entire nurturing stage can be automated to provide the potential client with relevant information based on their actions and behaviours on your website, interactions with emails that you have previously sent to them, or even responses to SMS messages.

As an example, if a potential client clicks on a particular link in an email that they have received from you, an automated marketing system can then deliver specific, customised content to them, whereas if they don't click on that particular link, the system can serve alternative information. Thereby, the content the system provides becomes relevant, timely and engaging, delivering exactly the information that the potential client is seeking to help them move into the decision stage of the client journey.

While email communication forms the backbone of nurturing, the actual assets (material) you use can be similar to those that support step 3 (engage), except that in the nurturing stage, the content will be more in-depth and specific to the client's needs. Assets can include eBooks, FAQ sheets, case studies and invitations to participate in webinars where relevant.

While communications are mainly sent directly to the client on a one-to-one basis utilising, for example, email or text messages, you can also remind them of your firm by serving relevant advertising to them as they browse other websites or scroll through their Facebook feeds. These ads should be tailored to the exact content they are interested in. For example, if the prospect has visited a particular page on your website, or shown an interest in a particular subject, you can present Facebook or Google Display advertisements to them that are directly related to the pages they viewed and actions they took.

STEP 5 – ONBOARD

Onboarding aligns with the decision stage of the client journey and occurs when a prospect makes a final decision and formally engages your firm's services.

You can assist potential clients to transition from the nurture to the onboarding step in a number of ways. For example, you can clarify any areas they are not clear on, provide pro-forma documentation or anything else that will assist them to finalise their decision.

Onboarding then involves the process of formally engaging the client, the execution of relevant documentation etc, and working closely with them to ensure you exceed their expectations from the outset. Again, marketing automation adds value to this step by streamlining and simplifying all interactions. For example, the process of creating, despatching and executing contracts can all be automated.

STEP 6 – IMPRESS

While your content and interactions throughout the previous five stages have created a positive impression of you and your services, leading the client to like and trust you, it is important to continue this momentum during and after engagement. The impress stage, therefore, becomes effective the minute a client engages your services, and continues after engagement is complete.

You need to deliver on your promises, but in today's environment, that alone is not sufficient. To impress, you need to wow your clients by delivering a remarkable experience, more than you promised and more than they expected. This stage aligns with the referral stage of the client journey. Happy, delighted and impressed clients are highly likely to not only engage your firm when they next need your type of services, but also recommend you to others.

STEP 7 – LOYALTY

The loyalty stage also aligns with the referral stage of the client journey.

Most businesses focus virtually exclusively on new client acquisition to the detriment of existing client retention. Engaging with existing clients by following up with them and maintaining an appropriate ongoing relationship will help ensure they continue to use you and refer others to you.

The level of this ongoing communication is dependent on the services you provided. It could simply be an email on the client's birthday, or legislative updates relevant to the services they received. Again, you can achieve this through automation that requires minimal to no time and effort on your part.

Summary

Potential clients move through the client journey on their way to engaging the services of a lawyer. This journey consists of three main stages prior to engagement – awareness, consideration and decision – and one post engagement stage – referral. The 7-Step Growth Blueprint is a clear and simple framework to help potential clients move through the client journey by providing them with appropriate communications and information at each stage.

The alignment of the 7-Step Growth Blueprint with the client journey is depicted in the following diagram (Figure 7.2).

By providing potential clients with relevant, personalised information at the right time, you can help them develop a connection with you, trust you, like you and recognise you as an expert on the subject matter relevant to their problem. As a result, they will be significantly more inclined to engage you as their first choice of legal services provider.

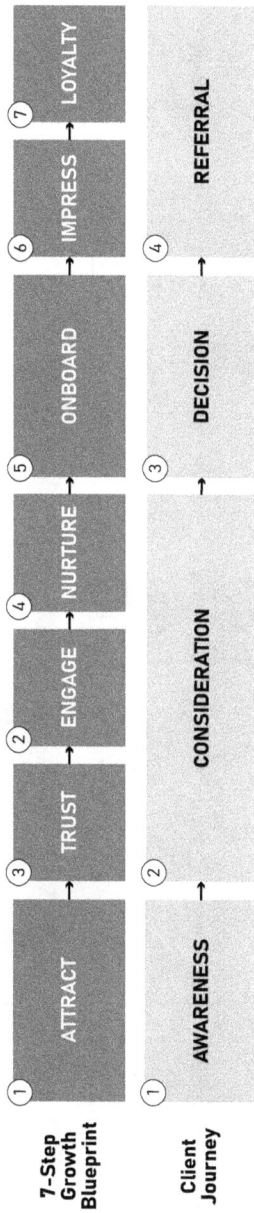

7-Step Growth Blueprint

1. ATTRACT
3. TRUST
2. ENGAGE
4. NURTURE
5. ONBOARD
6. IMPRESS
7. LOYALTY

Client Journey

1. AWARENESS
2. CONSIDERATION
3. DECISION
4. REFERRAL

Figure 7.2: Alignment of the 7-Step Growth Blueprint and Client Journey

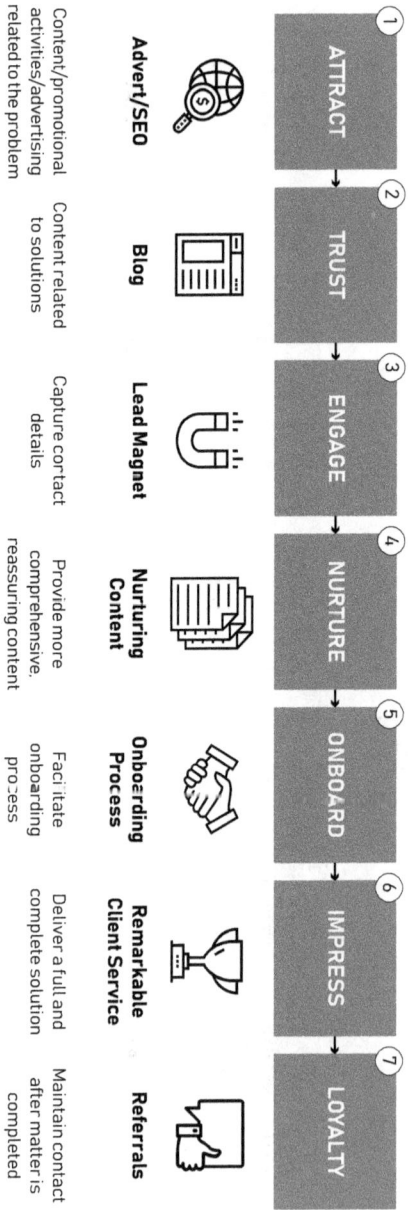

1 ATTRACT	2 TRUST	3 ENGAGE	4 NURTURE	5 ONBOARD	6 IMPRESS	7 LOYALTY
Advert/SEO	**Blog**	**Lead Magnet**	**Nurturing Content**	**Onboarding Process**	**Remarkable Client Service**	**Referrals**
Content/promotional activities/advertising related to the problem	Content related to solutions	Capture contact details	Provide more comprehensive, reassuring content	Facilitate onboarding process	Deliver a full and complete solution	Maintain contact after matter is completed

Figure 7.3: Content Strategy at Each Stage of the 7-Step Growth Blueprint

CHAPTER 8

Website

Introduction

Your website forms the central pillar around which you will develop many of your digital marketing initiatives. For example, when a potential client conducts a Google search, your listing that appears on Google's SERP will usually include a link to a landing page on your website. Similarly, any directory listings, Google ads and Facebook ads will generally be configured to link to relevant pages on your website.

Blogs, analytics, marketing automation systems, integrated appointment setting tools, contact details and other marketing systems, such as a client membership site, all require a website to leverage off for maximum benefit.

Today, a website is an essential component of a growth marketing strategy.

Key reasons for having a website

ENGAGING POTENTIAL CLIENTS

We have discussed the client journey at length, from awareness to consideration to decision, and ultimately referral. Your website plays an important role in engaging and moving potential clients through each stage of their client journey, with a view to them ultimately selecting you as their preferred lawyer.

Your website helps engage potential clients by:

- Showcasing your expertise
- Building your credibility
- Establishing trust in you
- Providing education
- Setting you apart from competitors
- Providing contact details

The first stage of a client's journey frequently begins with them taking one of the following actions:

- Clicking a link in a listing that has been returned in a Google search
- Clicking on an online advertisement, such as a display advertisement, search advertisement (pay per click), or social media advertisement
- Clicking on your firm's listing in a directory such as the local law society directory
- Clicking on a link in a social media post or article

These links need to take potential clients to your website where they can continue moving through the client journey.

In the absence of a website, you severely limit not only your digital marketing opportunities, resulting in many potential clients continuing to remain unaware of your firm, but also your ability to showcase your expertise and move clients through the client journey.

At its most basic level, your website provides potential clients with a resource that helps them:

- Find answers to many of their problems
- Learn about your expertise
- Understand the services you provide
- Understand your brand positioning
- Locate your contact details

Essentially, your website is a means for potential clients to conduct a large part of their research as they move through the client journey and finalise their engagement.

Potential clients will visit your website to validate you, checking that you legitimately offer the legal services they require and are a genuine option for consideration. Your website provides simple but important information such as contact details. It also provides a tangible public face to your firm 24/7, 365 days per year, giving potential clients confidence in you and your firm. The content on your website positions you as an authority in your field and helps establish trust in both you and your firm.

BRAND POSITIONING

Your website should reflect your unique selling points and positioning in the market. For example, if you are a suburban lawyer working with families, the look and feel of your website will be designed differently from that of a lawyer working with multinational corporates.

IMPROVED BUSINESS PROCESSES

Without a website, you are likely to receive time-consuming telephone calls or email requests for basic information, such as whether or not you provide the particular services a potential client requires. This type of contact is inefficient and can incur a significant cost in terms of both time and lost income.

If potential clients can obtain basic details from your website before contacting you, any telephone and email correspondence you ultimately have with them will be more effective and efficient, and have a higher likelihood of resulting in a new client engagement.

There are also many areas where a website can cut down on inefficient administration and business processing tasks. For example, you may be able to place contact forms on your website that will automatically record contact details directly into your internal management systems. These details can then be used to populate documents such as engagement agreements, cost schedules, NDAs etc.

One of the greatest timesavers that you can include on your website is a simple-to-use function for clients to check your availability and schedule appointments with you. These appointments can be held as online meetings, telephone meetings or face-to-face in your office. You can manually or automatically confirm each appointment, depending on your own preferences.

BLOGGING

Blogging is one of the most powerful ways to increase awareness of your firm and establish your credibility. You can link many of your social media posts and online advertisements to your blog posts. Blogging provides much of the free content that supports step 2 (trust) of the 7-Step Growth Blueprint. By creating, publishing and distributing useful content, you will position yourself as an authority in your field of expertise and differentiate yourself from the competition.

Your blog forms an integrated component of your website, and should include call-to-action buttons that link to relevant pages. Blogging improves your SEO, as well as provides a seamless process that supports your potential client's journey.

REMARKETING

Remarketing advertisements (advertisements displayed to previous visitors to your website) enable you to remind potential clients of your firm and your services if they have not yet followed up with you. While you may not yet have personal contact details for these potential clients, it is possible with remarketing to remain top of their mind by displaying online adverts to them as they browse other websites.

MARKETING AUTOMATION

Marketing automation, which we will discuss in detail in Chapter 9, is the technology that supports the progression of a potential client through the client journey. Your website tightly integrates with marketing automation systems to enable you to develop and deliver world-class growth strategies.

Types of websites

Business websites come in different forms and serve many different purposes. Some of the main types include:

- Brochure websites, which are essentially basic web pages with the same information presented to all visitors

- Ecommerce websites, on which clients can purchase or book products or services
- Websites that form the front-end (user interface) to databases and applications, such as a client centre

Website content can be static, such as brochure sites, or dynamic, such as when business applications are integrated and the site is continually updating.

Many law firm websites start out as brochure sites, but today, you can do so much more, easily and cost effectively, to help grow your firm exponentially. For example, consider integrated appointment setting, integrated document management systems, automated client engagement, and even client centres that clients can log into for case updates, general information, or to submit documents.

Considerations when developing your website

Over the years, websites have become easier and more affordable to build and maintain, and as internet technologies continue to improve, functionality and interactivity are improving exponentially. Features that once required teams of developers to design and document can now be achieved by non-programmers in minutes, using off-the-shelf plugins.

Likewise, just a few years ago, video over the internet was slow and often unusable, whereas today, video livestreaming and video conferencing is commonplace. Video is now one of the most effective forms of online marketing to engage with both potential and existing clients.

You need to give careful planning and consideration to your website design and development. Key areas for consideration include:

- Overall website objectives
- Domain names and page URLs
- Budget
- Technology platform
- Availability of web developers
- Ease of enhancements and content updates
- Hosting
- Integration with other technologies
- Mobile responsiveness (mobile-first approach)
- Site structure
- Content and page structure
- Copywriting and web design
- Search engine optimisation
- Google Analytics

The reason for highlighting these technical considerations is to ensure that you have a list of items for discussion with your web developer when you start developing or upgrading your website.

Let's look at each of the above considerations in a little more detail.

OVERALL WEBSITE OBJECTIVES

- Develop your site in a way that communicates and resonates appropriately with your specific client persona

- Position yourself and your firm as an authority in your field of expertise

- Ensure your website incorporates client acquisition features and functionality, for example, call-to-action buttons, social media share buttons, forms etc

- Design your website to provide features and functionality that support the 7-Step Growth Blueprint

- Incorporate business processes and marketing automation that increases client acquisition and improves business efficiencies, for example, online appointment scheduling, document management integration, CRM integration etc

DOMAIN NAME AND PAGE URLS

Your domain name (www.example.com) is usually the name of your firm. However, you may decide to use keywords, ie words that potential clients use when searching for your services, in your domain name, such as www.examplelawyer.com. Including keywords in domain names and URLs is an SEO ranking factor, although it's currently believed to be of relatively low value.

Domain names should be short and memorable. Avoid using numbers and hyphens wherever possible.

Purchase all appropriate domain name extensions, eg .com, .com.au, .net. Once you own them, it protects you from others registering the same domain name with different extensions. You can then register as many extensions as you desire and simply redirect them to your homepage.

Page URLs are the URLs specific to the various pages in your website. For example, www.examplelawyer .com/car-accident-compensation will take a visitor to your page that describes your services relating to motor vehicle accidents.

BUDGET

There are many factors that influence the cost of developing your website, including:

- The technology you use
- The web developer you engage (experience, technical expertise, freelancer, agency etc)
- Whether you engage a professional graphic designer, copywriter or SEO expert
- The specific functionality and complexity of the site

TECHNOLOGY PLATFORM

WordPress is currently the most popular content management system for new websites. There are many reasons for this, including:

- It is free open-source technology

- It is relatively easy and quick to develop a WordPress website compared to many other technologies

- It offers extensive functionality through prebuilt plugins

- There is a good availability of WordPress developers

- Ongoing content maintenance can be relatively simple and can generally be done in-house by non-technical staff

- It offers flexibility to build many different types of websites, from simple brochure sites through to more complex ecommerce and membership sites

If you do select WordPress to build your website in, I highly recommend incorporating plugins that offer the following core functionality:

- Security

- Back-up

- Caching

- Social media publishing

If you are using a standard off-the-shelf WordPress theme, it is important that your developer creates a child theme and builds your site on the child theme. This means that if there is a technical update to the theme, none of the customised code that your developer may have implemented will be impacted. In the absence of a child theme, WordPress updates could overwrite customisations, potentially rendering your website inoperable.

AVAILABILITY OF WEB DEVELOPERS

The availability and affordability of web developers is an important consideration. This is not so much a problem with WordPress, which has many developers and significant competition between them for work, but more so for the less popular website or enterprise level technologies, where there are fewer developers and less competition.

EASE OF ENHANCEMENTS AND CONTENT UPDATES

When you require website enhancements or content updates, it is important that you can do as much as possible using in-house resources, rather than engaging the services of a web developer. Again, this is generally not a problem with websites built using WordPress, but can become difficult when websites are developed in some of the other content management systems.

There are over 50,000 plugins in the WordPress repository. A plugin is essentially prebuilt software that is readily available and can be added to a WordPress website to add functionality. Rather than you needing to develop functionality specific to your site, you may find it has already been developed and is available as a plugin, saving you time and cost.

HOSTING

Your website will need to be hosted on a server. This is usually done through professional hosting companies using high-grade data centres.

When you're selecting a hosting provider, it is important to ensure they:

- Are cost effective
- Have a secure environment
- Host the specific technology your website is built in
- Have dedicated and responsive technical support for when issues arise
- Regularly back-up
- Maintain current hosting technologies and fast, high-quality servers

INTEGRATION WITH OTHER TECHNOLOGIES

If you wish to integrate your CRM, practice management, appointment scheduling, or any other third-party systems with your website for enhanced functionality, investigate this prior to deciding on a technology.

There are a number of ways to integrate separate systems, such as:

- Direct native integration
- Integration via an application program interface (API)
- Using various third-party middleware or bridging solutions

Not all systems can be integrated with other systems, so it is important to understand whether your current systems can, or should, be integrated with your website, and if so, what the most effective way to achieve this is.

MOBILE RESPONSIVENESS (MOBILE-FIRST APPROACH)

Over 50% of worldwide web traffic is now conducted using a mobile device. Google has also advised that mobile-responsive websites will receive favourable treatment in search engine enquiries.

Early websites were built to display on desktop computer screens, but as mobile devices became more popular, these sites did not suit them. The text became too small to read, and buttons and hyperlinks were difficult to click.

Responsive websites automatically adapt and alter their layout to suit the device they are being viewed on.

SITE STRUCTURE

A website's structure refers to how its individual pages are grouped together in sections and linked to each other to form the overall website.

The structure is important for two key reasons. Firstly, people need to be able to navigate the site and easily find the sections and content they are seeking. Secondly, Google's search engine crawlers need to be able to navigate their way through the site for the purpose of indexing.

The traditional website structure looks like a pyramid. At the top is your homepage, beneath it are category pages, and below them are subcategories. This is a hierarchical approach.

A recent development is the addition of hub and spoke pages to support SEO. This structure essentially consists of subject (hub) pages, which are comprehensive single pages covering an entire subject, and multiple topic (spoke) pages linking to each subject page. Each topic page probes into a particular topic introduced in the subject page. This linking structure indicates to search engines that the subject page is an authority on the subject it covers, and over time, the page may rank highly for that subject.

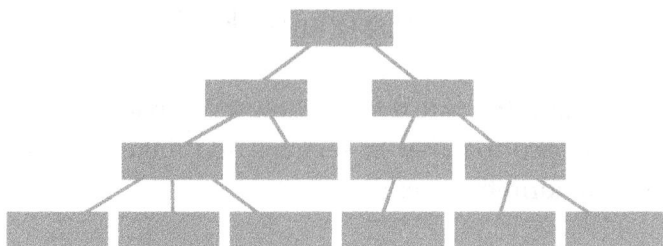

Figure 8.1: Traditional Website Structure

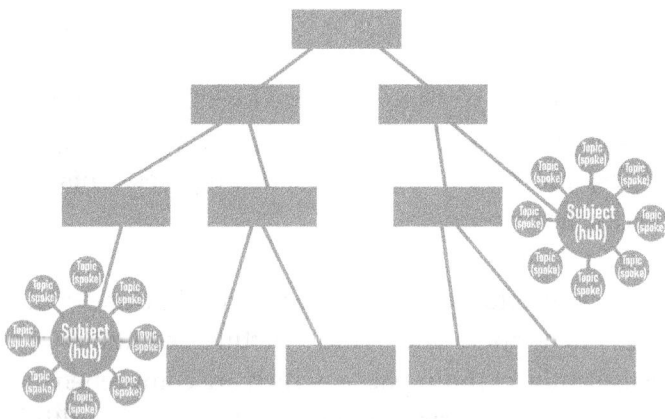

Figure 8.2: Website Structure with Subject and Topic Pages Added

CONTENT AND PAGE STRUCTURE

When you're developing a website, every page, as well as the site as a whole, needs an objective and purpose. To demonstrate page objectives, we will consider a home page versus a landing page.

The objective of a home page may, for example, be to provide a high-level introduction to your firm and motivate the visitor to delve further into the site to find more specific information. Home pages can have multiple outgoing links to other pages on your website.

A visitor generally arrives at a landing page after clicking on an advertisement, social media post or call to action on another page of the website. On a landing page, the visitor may be able to complete a form, download something of value, or read a blog article related to the social media post or advertisement.

Let's assume that the landing page is a simple blog article that the visitor has arrived at from a link in a social media post. Once they have read the blog article, the visitor may desire more in-depth information, in which case you will need to make sure a call-to-action button is available at the end of the blog article. This will take the reader to a dedicated landing page where they can enter their details and access the additional information.

Advertising is generally specific to a topic, so any visitors arriving on the website after clicking on an advert or conducting a Google search need to be taken directly to a landing page relating to the advertisement or the SERP listing, never the homepage. While a home page is broad, a landing page is specific.

COPYWRITING AND WEB DESIGN

The value of a good copywriter, particularly one who is familiar with SEO copywriting, and web designer cannot be underestimated. These are two important considerations to help ensure your website will appear in Google searches, engage potential clients, represent your brand appropriately and differentiate you from competitors.

Good copywriters understand that every page starts with a well-articulated value proposition that addresses the visitor's problem or question. The copy should then progress in a logical way, delivering on the objectives of the page.

Many copywriters structure their web page copy according to the AIDA formula – attention, interest, desire, action – while others use the PAS formula – problem, agitation, solution. Both structures are fairly self-explanatory, and are designed to elicit maximum engagement and action from the reader.

In addition to utilising a formal page structure, copywriters incorporate trust builders. Trust builders can be anything that helps a website visitor gain trust in you and move to the next step in the client journey, eg testimonials.

When you're engaging the services of a web copywriter, consider their understanding and ability to write SEO copy. SEO copywriting is both an art and a science. The structure of the copy – how, where and what words are used – together with your site's design plays a major role in determining the success of your site.

SEO copywriters understand and apply the key elements of copywriting that impact on SEO, eg copy length, keyword research, long- and short-tail keywords, heading hierarchy (H1, H2 etc), image alt tags (image labels read by search engines), and the myriad of other important SEO copywriting considerations.

A good web designer is also important. They understand that when they're designing a website, they must ensure their designs support both mobile and desktop devices, so engage a designer with experience across both. While there are many excellent graphic designers, not all have web design experience.

Depending on the stage your firm is at and your budget, you may elect to use a predesigned WordPress theme, which will minimise design costs while still being fully mobile responsive (depending on the theme you select).

SEARCH ENGINE OPTIMISATION (IN DETAIL)

Throughout this book, I have referred to the importance of SEO and Google Search. Entire books have been written on SEO alone, so I will limit this section to a highlight of some of the major considerations.

A search engine indexes every website, and when someone undertakes a search, its algorithm returns a list of websites in the order in which the algorithm ranks their relevance and authority. While Google has advised the importance of some ranking factors, such as mobile responsiveness, site speed and secure pages (HTTPS), the specific details of the vast majority of ranking factors are not publicly known. One reason for this 'secrecy' is that it stops manipulation of rankings, therefore ensuring the search engine displays the results most relevant to the potential client's search.

Google's algorithm is thought to consider over 200 ranking criteria, roughly segmented into three key categories:

- Technology
- Copywriting
- Backlinks

As a lawyer, your goal is to be as high as possible on the first page of the search results.

Technology

Website technology and its configuration play a crucial role in the optimisation of your website. It is generally considered that WordPress is SEO friendly. However, there are still many technical considerations you need to address, even in a WordPress site. For example, an excessive number of plugins that can slow site speed, high-resolution imagery, poor hosting, non-mobile responsive technology, broken links and poor coding all impact negatively on your website's SEO.

Rather than include a comprehensive list of technical ranking factors here, which would probably take up an entire chapter on its own, I want to highlight a few of the better known ones. A mobile-responsive website, ie a website that automatically changes its layout in order to display most effectively on any size display, be it a desktop monitor, tablet or phone device, is an important ranking factor. You need to consider it a prerequisite for a well-performing SEO website.

Google has also advised that the speed of your site is an important ranking factor. Google's objective is to present the most relevant sites that not only include appropriate content, but also function well. A fast website is a major consideration in determining this. You can use Google's PageSpeed Insights tool to determine whether or not your website loading speed is acceptable. The faster the site, the more favourably Google views it. A page is generally expected to load in under two seconds. Page size, file types, website technology, hosting, traffic volume, connection speed etc are some of the main factors that will impact on page speed.

In addition to speed and mobile responsiveness, other known technology-related considerations that have an impact on SEO include:

- Robots.txt file

- XML sitemap

- Broken links

- Image alt text

- Deprecated HTML tags
- Page redirections
- Duplicate content
- JavaScript
- Page size
- HTTPS
- Images
- Google Console

Robots.txt file. A robots.txt file gives instructions to search engine robots on how to crawl and index pages.

XML sitemap. An extensible markup language (XML) sitemap is a file that lists all of your website's pages and is used to help search engines index them. You need to create XML sitemaps and submit them to Google.

Broken links. Broken links in a website are believed to have a detrimental effect on a site's SEO. Search engines crawl websites via their links in order to rank them. Broken links impact on a search engine's ability to crawl your site and therefore should be addressed.

SEO-friendly URLs. Use an SEO-friendly URL structure that includes keywords.

Image alt text. Search engine robots cannot read images. However, by including keywords in alt text (the words that appear when you scroll over an image), you can ensure search engines are able to understand what the image is and use it as a ranking factor.

Deprecated HTML tags. This is old-style coding that has become obsolete and should be removed from your website.

Page redirections. Pages that are redirected should have specific types of redirects set up to pass the SEO value of the source page to the destination page. These are usually known as 301 redirects.

Duplicate content. Google doesn't like duplicate content on a website as it becomes difficult to ascertain which is the more appropriate page to index and return in a search. Ideally, you need to eliminate duplicate content, but there may be times when you can't help but have duplicate content on different pages. In this instance, you can advise Google which page to index by including canonical links in the less appropriate page. A canonical link is short piece of code that tells Google that there is a more appropriate page to index than the one it has found.

JavaScript. Since 2014, Google has suggested that its technology is getting better at rendering or understanding JavaScript websites. However, Google does acknowledge that things don't always go according to plan, and that sometimes the JavaScript may be too complex, or even remove content from the page, which prevents it from being indexed.

Page size. The larger the page size, the slower the page speed and the longer the loading time. Page size essentially refers to the total file size of a page, eg 900KB, 3MB etc. File types such as video, high resolution images, audio etc can have a significant impact on page size.

HTTPS. Google advises that having a security certificate on your site plays a positive role when its algorithm is ranking your website. The url of websites with security certificates begin with https://

Images. Incorporate copy that needs to be read by search engine crawlers within the html code of a page rather than embodied within the actual images wherever possible.

Google Console. Includes tools that help you to improve your website's performance on Google Search. They also help you to measure traffic to your site, and identify and fix problems.

SEO copywriting

In addition to technical SEO considerations, there are a number of SEO ranking factors related to copywriting.

Some of the major copywriting considerations include, but are not limited to:

- Copy length
- Keywords
- Page context

- Meta tags
- Heading structure and hierarchy
- Link anchor text
- Page titles
- Image alt tags
- Internal and external links
- URL structure and words used

Copy length. In general, longer copy pages with more words, substance and relevance tend to perform better. However, this needs to be balanced with user experience.

Keywords. Page content should incorporate keywords identified in your keyword research, ie common words or phrases website visitors use when they're searching for information related to your services. Keywords can be classified as long-tail keywords, ie phrases of three or more words, and short-tail keywords, ie single words. Long-tail keywords are generally more relevant and effective than short-tail keywords.

Page context. Google is becoming smarter at understanding the context of a website and its pages without having to base its understanding exclusively on the number of times specific keywords are used. For example, Google now recognises synonyms, related words and the general message presented on a page. It is, however, still important to conduct research into keywords and incorporate them, and variations of them, into your content in a structured and methodical way.

Meta tags. Meta tags such as meta description and meta title are snippets of text within the page code that explain the page content. While search engines may no longer consider meta tags for page ranking, they still play an important role. For example, the meta description tag is used by Google to display a description of the web page in its SERP. A well-written, relevant meta description increases the likelihood of a potential client clicking through to your website from the search engine results page.

Heading structure and hierarchy. Heading structure and hierarchy relates to how headings such as H1, H2, H3 etc are used and structured on each page. It is recommended that a single H1 heading be used per page.

Link anchor text. These are the words used in link text and should incorporate or relate to keywords where possible.

Page titles. Page titles are the names given to each page.

Image alt tags. These are the words that will sometimes appear when you scroll over an image on a website.

Internal and external links.

URL structure and words used.

In addition to carefully considering the layout, structure and content of each page, you need to consider the overall structure of the website. New websites are starting to incorporate the hub and spoke style structure to support SEO. An example of a hub and spoke structure for a law firm would be a main subject (hub) page that addresses, in general, all the different types of personal injury claims and provides an overview of each. The site can then elaborate on specific types of personal injury in dedicated topic (spoke) pages that are linked exclusively to the subject page.

Backlinks (inbound links)

The third major component of successful SEO is a solid backlinking strategy. Google advises that incoming links to your website (backlinks) from relevant and appropriate websites will positively impact on your ranking. If another website is linking to yours, Google considers your site to be relevant and important in some way, and ranks it accordingly.

Having said that, not all backlinks have a positive effect. In fact, some backlinks can be detrimental to your SEO ranking. Google is smart enough to recognise whether your backlinks are from high-quality, appropriate and relevant websites. The quality of the sites is based on a score, known as site authority, that Google applies to all websites. The higher the authority of the website linking to your site, the more beneficial it is to your ranking. Links from sites with low authority have minimal impact, while links from link farms, low-value directories or spurious websites will have a detrimental effect on your ranking.

Link building is a long-term strategy, but it can pay high dividends and be worth the effort. My advice is to build relationships with other highly relevant, credible and legitimate sites in the industry and negotiate incoming links from these sites.

While negotiating these relationships, you can also create listings in respected online directories, such as *True Local*, *Yelp*, relevant association directories and Google My Business, etc. These listings will all link back to your site. Be aware, though, that there are a number of low-quality directories that have been created for the sole purpose of selling backlinks. Google recognises these sites and any links from them can have a detrimental effect on your ranking. It is extremely important to avoid low-quality directories and only have backlinks from legitimate, relevant and high-quality sites.

Make sure your social media profiles and your social media posts link back to your website where possible. Creating a blog on your website can also help boost incoming links considerably. As readers share and link back to your blogposts from their websites, so your inbound links will increase in number.

SEO tools

There are a number of tools that analyse websites and score many of the SEO ranking factors to help identify areas where you can make improvements. Below are some of the tools I have used.

Free tools:

- https://seositecheckup.com
- https://gtmetrix.com
- https://website.grader.com
- https://search.google.com/search-console/about

Paid tools:

- https://semrush.com
- https://moz.com
- https://ahrefs.com

Outsourcing your SEO

Should you decide to outsource your SEO initiatives, it is important to select a supplier with care and due diligence. Many SEO practitioners focus on one or two of the three main categories affecting SEO performance. As such, it is unlikely that a technical SEO practitioner will be able to draft high-quality copy, while an SEO copywriter is unlikely to have the technical skills of an SEO programmer.

The above commentary is a high-level overview of SEO. While incredibly important, SEO is a relatively slow and long-term strategy that takes time to pay dividends. However, when it does, the dividends can be well worth the effort and resources you will have invested.

GOOGLE ANALYTICS

Google Analytics is a free tool that provides insights into the performance of your website and the behaviour of your website visitors.

For example, Google Analytics helps you understand how visitors are arriving on your site, whether it be from your Google or Facebook advertising, social media posts, organic Google searches, other websites, or by directly keying your domain name into their browser. You can identify which pages are most popular, how long visitors are spending on each page, their flow through your site, the countries and locations they are originating from, and whether they are new or repeat visitors.

Google Analytics also provides insights into the devices your website visitors are using, for example whether they're visiting from desktop computers, tablets or mobile phones. It then drills in further to identify operating systems and other metrics that are important in helping you develop and maintain the most effective website possible. Other useful stats include the age and gender of website visitors.

Google Analytics doesn't report on or identify individual users, but rather presents an aggregated view of all website visitors. Google Analytics also integrates with Google Ads and Google Search Console.

MISCELLANEOUS ITEMS

When you're developing your website, there are a number of important items that many developers don't include unless you specifically request them.

Ensure your developer does the following:

- Creates a Google Analytics account and adds the Google tracking code to your website
- Creates and configures Google Console (previously known as Webmaster Tools)
- Links your Google Console, Google Ads and Google Analytics accounts
- Adds your Facebook pixel code to your website

Summary

A website is a necessity for any modern law firm. Without it, a firm cannot be serious about generating growth.

A website will help you position your brand, attract, nurture and win new clients, and improve efficiencies. It forms the backbone of a modern digital marketing strategy and enables you to combine all the various components of digital marketing into an effective growth marketing solution.

Key areas to consider when you're developing your website include:

- Overall website objectives
- Domain names and page URLs
- Budget
- Technology platform
- Availability of web developers
- Ease of enhancements and content updates
- Hosting
- Integration with other technologies
- Mobile responsiveness (mobile-first approach)
- Site structure
- Content and page structure
- Copywriting and web design
- Search engine optimisation
- Google Analytics

The absence of a website in your marketing ecosystem would be akin to having roads, traffic lights, petrol stations and parking lots, but not having the cars to link them all together to maximise the value of each component.

CHAPTER 9

Marketing Automation

Introduction

Congratulations on making it to this final chapter! This is the most exciting section of the book.

Marketing automation technology leverages every component of the marketing ecosystem, enabling you to execute the 7-Step Growth Blueprint effectively. It provides the fuel that ignites your marketing strategy and drives growth.

The technologies and methodologies we will discuss in this chapter were originally the exclusive domain of large organisations and corporations with significant marketing budgets, technical resources and marketing personnel. Over the years, the cost and complexity of the technology has reduced enormously, and new, easy-to-use, highly functional systems have been designed specifically for smaller and medium-sized firms. In fact, they are now so affordable that even sole operators can use marketing automation to help scale and grow at an accelerated rate.

What is marketing automation?

Marketing automation helps you amplify your lead generation activities and convert more leads into paying clients by automating many of the processes in the 7-Step Growth Blueprint. Essentially, it can help you to grow your firm while you sleep, 24/7, 365 days per year.

With modern marketing automation systems, you position yourself as an authority, streamline your marketing activities, automate repetitive but time-consuming tasks, and generate personalised responses to potential clients, based on their actions, interests and current position in the 7-Step Growth Blueprint (attract, trust, engage, nurture, onboard, impress and loyalty). Marketing automation interacts and communicates with potential clients in a relevant, personalised and timely manner.

By automating resource-intense marketing processes, you can get on with running your firm, while your marketing automation system develops your credibility, engages and nurtures potential clients, and in some cases, even onboards them. Furthermore, by integrating your marketing automation system with your internal systems wherever possible, you can not only take your marketing to new levels, but you can also streamline many of your internal business processes.

To demonstrate, let's have a look at an example of how marketing automation can generate more clients and improve internal process efficiencies.

A potential client becomes aware that they have a problem and begins researching it on Google. A link to one of your blogs appears near the top of the Google SERP, and the potential client (whom you are not yet even aware of) clicks on the link and is taken directly to your blog article.

They read the blog article which demonstrates your understanding of their issue and expert ability to help them. It also raises further questions that they need to consider. Within the body of the blog, as well as at the end, are call-to-action buttons linking to a more comprehensive eBook that provides additional answers and depth to their research. Having developed a greater level of confidence and trust in you and your firm, they click on the call-to-action button and are taken to a dedicated landing page on your website where they enter their details to access the eBook.

The marketing automation system recognises the content they are interested in and records this, along with details such as their name and email address. You now have a record of the potential client and are aware of their main interests.

The marketing automation system emails them a link to download the eBook. A couple of hours later, after reading the eBook, they return to your website and view additional pages. The marketing automation system records the pages they visit and automatically sends them personalised communications specific to the content on those pages. The potential client is delighted with the additional information and appreciates the help and value you are providing.

Your marketing automation system has recorded their actions, interests and behaviours and based on this automatically sends the potential client an invitation to schedule an initial free, no-obligation thirty-minute telephone discussion. The invitation includes a link to your scheduling system that shows your availability and allows them to book a time to call. When they book the call, the system enters it into your diary. Ten minutes before the call, the potential client automatically receives a text message from you, reminding them of the call. The entire process has been automated, again without any additional time or effort from yourself.

During the call, the potential client decides they would like to work with you, but needs to see a cost schedule first. You record this request in your marketing automation system, which in this case has been integrated with your document management system, and the relevant document is automatically populated and emailed to them for review.

This example demonstrates how automation can help you increase authority and win clients with virtually no additional effort on your part. The automation workflows, known as funnels, can include a number of communications over a long period of time, or, where time is of the essence, fewer communications over a short period, even within a single day. The automation process is cost effective, and most importantly, can result in new clients that you would never have obtained without marketing automation.

Now let's have a look at the main components of a marketing automation system.

CRM

CRM stands for customer relationship management (or in our case, client relationship management) and is a core component of the marketing automation system. The CRM system stores client and potential client details, segments clients, records their interactions, behaviours and interests, and populates automated communications with relevant content.

In addition to standard information such as name, address, email and phone number, a CRM system can also record client actions and behaviours such as the pages they've visited on your website, whether they've clicked on links in emails you've sent them and documents they've downloaded. Additionally, tasks, notes, matter details, scheduled follow-ups, and much more can be recorded in the CRM.

The data stored in the CRM system is used to manage existing relationships and proactively nurture and educate potential clients. The CRM system tracks all contact and communication history, and ensures every interaction is personalised and customised.

You can manually enter information directly into a CRM system, have it automatically entered via integrated third-party applications, or potential clients can themselves enter information via forms on your website. In the example above, the potential client entered their details to download the eBook, and all of those details were recorded in the CRM system, as were the meeting details when they scheduled their appointment.

You may already be using a CRM system in your firm. Depending on your system, it may be possible to integrate the marketing automation CRM with your existing CRM to ensure the data you have in your current system is reflected in the marketing automation system. In other cases, you may simply decide to use the marketing automation system's CRM to replace other internal systems. This decision will be dependent on your firm's objectives, requirements and existing practices.

While all CRM systems differ in their specific features and functionality, those common to most include:

- Fields and custom fields
- Notes, appointments and documents
- Web profile

- Campaigns
- Reporting

FIELDS AND CUSTOM FIELDS

CRM systems consist of client records, more commonly referred to as contact records. If you have 100 clients, you would have at least 100 contact records. Each contact record stores information relevant to the contact, eg address, email, social media contact details, tasks, appointments, notes etc.

Standard information in a contact record is stored in fields. The address section, for example, could comprise of street name and number, suburb, postcode/zip code, and country fields.

Every firm has differing needs from a CRM system. To provide flexibility, in addition to the standard system fields, many CRM systems enable you to create custom fields to store specific information. For example, you may wish to create custom fields to store information such as reference number, matter, resolution date, compensation amount, beneficiaries, executors etc.

Fields can also be used to personalise and customise outgoing communications to clients by merging the unique contents of each field into the clients' communications. Any data in standard or custom fields in the CRM system can generally be merged into communications. For example, the first name field can be merged into an email to enable it to begin with 'Dear (first name)'.

The data within both standard and custom fields can also be used to segment the client database in order to more effectively engage with particular client groups. For example, let's assume you offer both family and personal injury services. You may decide to develop dedicated communications for family services clients, and an alternative set of communications only relevant to personal injury clients.

NOTES, APPOINTMENTS AND DOCUMENTS

The notes section of the CRM system is important for recording information that is not captured within the contact or custom fields. For example, you may have a phone conference with a client and need to record the details of the call in the client's record. The notes section enables you to do so and access the information at any time.

The CRM system's appointment recording functionality records details such as date, time and location. Appointments are generally recorded in chronological order by date. The contents of appointment-related fields can frequently be merged into reminder email or text (SMS) messages.

Many CRM systems provide the ability to store documents relevant to a specific client or potential client in that client's contact record for easy access.

WEB PROFILE

In the example at the beginning of the chapter, the potential client visited the website on a number of occasions. When a CRM system is part of an integrated marketing automation solution, all of the potential client's interactions, such as the pages they've viewed and the time spent on each page, can be recorded. This helps you identify their interests, segment them and communicate with them in a more informed and personalised manner.

CAMPAIGNS

When you're using a single integrated marketing auto-mation solution with its own CRM system, there will be deep, streamlined integration and communication between the functionality of the marketing campaign module and the CRM module. In essence, the two modules function as a single unified system.

While integration between the marketing campaign module and the CRM system delivers wide-ranging benefits over independent systems, the most notable is the ability to capture and record a contact's details, behaviours and actions to develop highly personalised and customised campaigns. For example, if a contact clicks a specific link in an email, visits a particular web-site page, or schedules an appointment, these actions (along with many others) will be recorded in the CRM system and can trigger personalised communications.

REPORTING

Using an integrated CRM system, you benefit from both standard and customised reporting. You can report on virtually anything you record in the CRM system, for example, your highest revenue clients, most popular services, largest compensation payouts, value of properties settled or country of origin of clients you've provided immigration support services to.

Automated campaign builder

Depending on the marketing automation system you choose, the automated campaign builder may have different names, such as campaign builder or automation workflows. For the purpose of this book, I'll refer to it as the automated campaign builder.

The automated campaign builder is the main area within the marketing automation software where customised and personalised client communications and interactions are created, eg the landing pages that potential clients arrive on after clicking on an advertisement or call-to-action button. Marketing campaigns created in the builder can include personalised emails based on a potential client's position in the client journey, or actions they have taken on your website.

The automated campaign builder also manages, measures and tracks real-time campaign statistics and reporting such as landing page performance and email open and click-through rates. These are incredibly important stats to analyse as they allow you to fine-tune campaigns to maximise the growth of your firm.

The automated campaign builder creates campaigns specifically to engage with potential clients in a manner that is relevant to the stage they are at in their client journey.

TACTICS FOR THE AWARENESS STAGE

When a potential client is in the awareness stage, you need to ensure you become known and visible to them. Common tactics for achieving this include advertising, SEO and blogging. Marketing automation enables you to maximise the benefits you derive from these acquisition methods.

Advertising integration

While your advertisements are each created in their own respective media platforms, eg Google Ads or Facebook, marketing automation systems integrate with them or complement them to maximise the advertising results.

For example, when your marketing automation system integrates with Facebook lead ads, it can automatically create a contact record in your CRM system when a potential client clicks on the advertisement. The information it adds to the record includes, at a minimum, the potential client's name and email address. At the same time, it can send an auto-response email to the potential client with further information relating to the subject promoted in the advertisement.

Depending on the potential client's level of engagement with your email, your marketing automation system may execute an ongoing drip nurturing campaign consisting of a number of emails over a period of time, ensuring the potential client remains aware of your firm.

SEO

Some marketing automation systems include tools to help improve your SEO. However, should you select a marketing automation system that does not natively include SEO management tools, there are numerous third-party tools available that achieve similar outcomes. A list of some of these tools is included in Chapter 8.

If you are using a WordPress website, I highly recommend that you install the Yoast SEO plugin to provide real-time guidance on optimising your content as it is written.

Blogs

Blogs are an important component of any acquisition campaign, and can actually be created within some marketing automation systems. Furthermore, once you've created your blog on you website, it can be automatically scheduled and posted to your various social media platforms at the most appropriate time.

Performance reporting

Once your blog is posted, sophisticated reporting identifies which online channels or social media accounts are driving the most visitors to your site. This helps identify which blogs and social strategies provide the highest response and ROI.

TACTICS FOR THE CONSIDERATION STAGE

Once a potential client has become aware of your firm and developed sufficient trust in you to provide their contact details, you can begin assisting them through the consideration stage. This is where you are able to provide automated, personalised, relevant and timely communications to help and nurture them based on their specific needs.

Landing pages

Many marketing automation systems enable you to create landing pages within the software itself. These pages can function as either standalone pages with their own domain, or they can be integrated into your website.

Landing pages differ from standard website pages in their purpose and structure. They have one single objective, which is generally to encourage a potential client to complete the form on the page to receive something in return, such as an eBook, event registration etc. By completing the form in the landing page, the potential client automatically logs their details in your CRM system. You can then use these details to trigger a nurturing campaign.

Lead capture forms

Lead capture forms are the actual forms themselves and can be used to achieve the same objective as landing pages, ie enable visitors to provide their details to receive content, register for an event etc.

The difference between a landing page and lead capture form is that a landing page usually includes the form on it, whereas a lead capture form is just the form itself. It can be embedded into a new or existing website page or displayed as a pop-up form over a page.

Automated processes

Once a website visitor has completed your form and become a lead in your CRM system, you can start communicating with them. With automation, you can identify which web pages they have viewed, the order in which they have viewed these pages, and the time they've spent on each. Using this knowledge (and the details the potential client submitted in the lead forms), you can set up workflows that automatically communicate appropriate content to them. For example, you can send customised emails relevant to their unique interests and behaviours on your website.

Identifying your website visitors

Google Analytics provides a lot of information on visitors to your website, but it is aggregated and anonymous, ie you cannot identify which pages a specific potential client has been to, how long they stayed on the page, or their journey from page to page. With marketing automation, once a visitor has completed a lead capture form and their details have been automatically entered into your CRM system, you can identify their individual activity on your website. For example, you can record the pages they have visited, their navigation through your site, the forms they've submitted, and anything they've downloaded. Knowing their individual interests based on their behaviours and actions on your website, you can then create automated communications that nurture them with highly personalised content.

Video views

When a potential client has viewed a video on your website, your automated marketing system can send them relevant communications based on whether they viewed the entire video or simply the first few seconds.

If they watched the entire video on a particular subject, an automated campaign could, for example, send them follow-up information, whereas if they only watched a few seconds, the campaign could send them a reminder to watch the rest of it.

Evergreen webinars

While many of us don't particularly enjoy live public speaking or presenting online webinars, they are two of the most effective ways to become known as an authority in your industry and attract potential clients. Evergreen webinars enable you to create recorded webinars which run at predetermined times, eg every Thursday at 6pm, or are dynamically timed, where timeslots are offered to a potential client based on when they register, eg registration time plus fifteen minutes. A potential client registers for a webinar and books the next convenient session. This means that every potential client could be viewing a webinar in their own unique time slot.

Google reviews

Google reviews are regularly checked by potential clients before they make a commitment to purchase or engage a service provider, and marketing automation offers a great opportunity to maximise your positive reviews. It does this by sending an email to clients once their matter has been completed that includes a simple question regarding their level of satisfaction with your service. Clients who respond positively then receive an automated email requesting they post a Google review. The email includes within it a link for them to click to leave their review.

Lead scoring

Lead scoring allows you to score and rank potential clients on the likelihood that they are ready to engage with you. The marketing automation system automatically scores their actions and behaviours and applies the appropriate number of points to each. Once a lead reaches a predefined score, you can categorise them as a potential client ready to engage, and you or the most appropriate person in your firm can contact them if necessary.

Lead sources

Lead sources allow you to record how a lead originally became aware of your firm, eg from a Google, Facebook or newspaper advertisement. This enables you to track your most effective advertising and which media generates the highest return on investment.

Email marketing

Marketing automation enables you to personalise, customise and time your emails to each potential client based on their previous interactions, personal details and specific requirements. Unlike email newsletters, where the same content is distributed to a mass audience at a specific time, marketing automation can deliver emails that are highly relevant, personalised and timely, thereby maximising engagement.

TACTICS FOR THE DECISION STAGE

Once a potential client is ready to engage your services, your onboarding processes need to be as seamless and efficient as possible. Modern online tools such as scheduling systems, document management software, client portals etc integrate with marketing automation solutions, ensuring that your potential client's records are automatically updated in the CRM system as they are being onboarded.

Online chat

Online chat is the sending and receiving of text messages in real time between potential clients and your firm using an instant messaging application on your computer or mobile device. It is rapidly becoming a popular means of communication between businesses and clients, with an increasing number of websites incorporating chat boxes in the bottom right corner of the page. These online chat boxes can be set to 'on' when they're being monitored or 'off' when they're not monitored. When they are not monitored, the potential client can still use them to send a message as an email to a nominated email address at the firm. The sender will be advised to expect a response via email.

Many online chat systems integrate with marketing automation CRM systems, ensuring that a record of chat correspondence is saved against each client's record.

Online appointment scheduling

Online appointment scheduling enables potential clients to schedule meetings with you based on your available timeslots. This can be via a booking page on your website, or a private link to the appointment setting interface that is emailed to potential clients. Again, many appointment scheduling systems integrate seamlessly with marketing automation solutions, ensuring appointments are tracked within the CRM system.

Confirmed appointments can automatically trigger actions such as notifying relevant internal partners or staff that the meeting has been scheduled. If the booking system is integrated with staff calendars, it can populate their calendar with details of the meeting.

Emails and SMS reminders can be configured to be sent to the client or potential client at predetermined times, eg as soon as the appointment is scheduled, twenty-four hours prior to the meeting, and finally one hour before the meeting.

Impress your clients

Automating workflow processes during onboarding and engagement not only delights the client, demonstrating your professionalism and proficiency, it also ensures you stay on top of the paperwork.

An excellent example of automating your workflow is integrating your document management system with your marketing automation and CRM system, enabling relevant documents to be automatically personalised and distributed to clients at the right time. Clients can then take action on those documents (eg execute them) and return them to you. This can all be achieved automatically without your additional involvement. Examples of such documents could be fee schedules, contracts or applications.

Integrating SMS with your marketing automation solution to notify clients of important actions and requirements is another valuable step in not only impressing them, but also reducing your overheads and becoming more efficient.

Summary

No matter how large or small your firm, if you're not leveraging marketing automation, you're not maximising your growth. A modern automation system is the fuel that ignites your marketing campaigns, amplifies your lead generation activities, and maximises client acquisition by:

- Getting you known by potential clients who need your help
- Helping potential clients solve their problems 24/7, 365 days per year
- Ensuring the right messages are sent to the right people at the right time
- Positioning you as a trusted authority
- Improving business process workflows and efficiencies
- Automating repetitive, time-consuming tasks and business processes
- Automating the underlying processes of the 7-Step Growth Blueprint (attract, trust, engage, nurture, onboard, impress and referral)

Marketing automation systems include sales, marketing and CRM functionality, automated communications, campaign workflows, external systems integration, and so much more. I highly recommend that you take advantage of marketing automation and implement strategies, tools and techniques that have been proven to be effective worldwide. Used well, they help boost your results and turbocharge your initiatives.

This brings us to the end of our journey into the many ways marketing can take your law firm to new and exciting levels of success. I hope you have found the strategies outlined in this book helpful and informative, and if you would like to explore the topics we have covered in *How To Grow Your Law Firm* further, please get in touch via www.growmylawfirm.com.au

Research

Below is a list of interesting references used during the research for this book.

Moschella D (2017) 'Digital Takes Aim at the Professions – Disrupting Doctors, Lawyers, Academics and Accountants', www.computerweekly.com/opinion /Digital-takes-aim-at-the-professions-disrupting -doctors-lawyers-academics-and-accountants

QLTS (2015) 'Top 5 Challenges Facing Lawyers Today', www.qlts.com/blog/profession/top-lawyers -challenges

Attorney General's Department (1995) 'Chapter 3: Lawyers', in *The Justice Statement*, www.austlii.edu.au /austlii/articles/scm/jchap3.html

Ryan E (2017) 'Former Top-tier Partner Launches "Australian-first" Multidisciplinary Firm', www .lawyersweekly.com.au/sme-law/22228-former -top-tier-partner-launches-australian-first -multidisciplinary-firm

Gilbert + Tobin (2016) 'G+T Increases Stake in Legal-Vision', www.gtlaw.com.au/news/gt-increases-stake
-legalvision

The Law Society of NSW, Commission of Inquiry (2017) *FLIP – The Future of Law and Innovation in the Profession*, www.lawsociety.com.au/advocacy-and
-resources/advocacy/flip

The Law Society of Western Australia (2017) *The Future of the Legal Profession*, www.lawsocietywa.asn
.au/wp-content/uploads/2015/10/2017DEC12-Law
-Society-Future-of-the-Legal-Profession.pdf

Australian Consumer Law (2010) 'Legislation: The Australian Consumer Law', http://consumerlaw.gov
.au/the-australian-consumer-law/legislation

Acknowledgements

A massive thank you to everyone in the legal industry who contributed their time and advice to the development of this book, particularly to my friend and highly experienced lawyer John Makris, for the vast amount of time and incredibly valuable feedback that he provided.

Thanks also to the team at Rethink Press, who provided invaluable support and assistance through every stage of the publishing process – Lucy McCarraher and Joe Gregory for their professional advice and inspiration, Alison Jack for her amazing editing skills, Kathleen Steeden for outstanding project management and Jane Smith for a perfect cover design.

And last but not least, to my partner Helen Smith, without whose ongoing support and encouragement this book would never have been possible, thank you so much.

The Author

Gerald Chait is a highly experienced marketing expert with a proven track record and a unique depth of knowledge across both traditional and digital marketing.

Not only has he generated incredible results for some of the largest national and multinational organisations, including Optus, Sharp Electronics and Reckon (QuickBooks), but he has also worked with numerous small/medium-sized businesses, and now runs his own successful consulting business.

Gerald is a certified partner of a number of the world's largest marketing automation technology suppliers, and maintains partnership status with many other technology organisations across the globe. Widely recognised for developing and leading high-performing marketing teams, he is respected for his excellent strategic and operational capabilities, as well as his creative entrepreneurial mindset, well-developed business acumen and proven results.

Always current with the latest marketing strategies, technologies and trends, he is one of the few strategic marketers who enjoys rolling his sleeves up and getting the tactical job done. He has a deep knowledge of marketing automation, content marketing, social media marketing, web development, SEO, digital advertising, direct mail as well as traditional marketing strategies.

Gerald's excellent results, combined with his core values of honesty, ethics and transparency before all else, have resulted in his building highly successful long-term client relationships.

www.ingramcontent.com/pod-product-compliance
Lightning Source LLC
Chambersburg PA
CBHW070352200326
41518CB00012B/2213